21ST CENTURY COMMUNICATION

LISTENING, SPEAKING, AND CRITICAL THINKING

4

CHRISTIEN LEE

NATIONAL GEOGRAPHIC LEARNING

CENGAGE Learning

Australia • Brazil • Mexico • Singapore • United Kingdom • United States

NATIONAL GEOGRAPHIC LEARNING | **CENGAGE Learning**

21st Century Communication: Listening, Speaking, and Critical Thinking
Student Book 4
Christien Lee

Publisher: Sherrise Roehr

Executive Editor: Laura Le Dréan

Managing Editor: Jennifer Monaghan

Senior Development Editor: Mary Whittemore

Associate Development Editor: Lisl Trowbridge

Media Research: Leila Hishmeh

Director of Global and U.S. Marketing: Ian Martin

Product Marketing Manager: Anders Bylund

Sr. Director, Production: Michael Burggren

Manager, Production: Daisy Sosa

Content Project Manager: Mark Rzeszutek

Senior Digital Product Manager: Scott Rule

Manufacturing Planner: Mary Beth Hennebury

Interior Design: Brenda Carmichael

Compositor: SPi Global

For product information and technology assistance, contact us at
Cengage Learning Customer & Sales Support, cengage.com/contact

For permission to use material from this text or product,
submit all requests online at **cengage.com/permissions**
Further permissions questions can be emailed to
permissionrequest@cengage.com

Student Book:
ISBN: 978-1-305-95547-9

Student Book with Online Workbook Sticker Code:
ISBN: 978-1-337-27583-5

National Geographic Learning
20 Channel Center Street
Boston, MA 02210
USA

National Geographic Learning, a Cengage Learning Company, has a mission to bring the world to the classroom and the classroom to life. With our English language programs, students learn about their world by experiencing it. Through our partnerships with National Geographic and TED, they develop the language and skills they need to be successful global citizens and leaders.

Locate your local office at **international.cengage.com/region**

Visit National Geographic Learning online at **NGL.cengage.com**
Visit our corporate website at **www.cengage.com**

Printed in the United States of America
Print Number: 01 Print Year: 2016

Reviewers

The authors and publisher would like to thank the following teachers from all over the world for their valuable input during the development process of the 21st Century Communication series.

Coleeta P. Abdullah, *EducationKSA, Saudi Arabia*

Ghada Al Attar, *AMIDEAST, Yemen*

Yazeed Al Jeddawy, *AMIDEAST, United Kingdom*

Zubidah Al Sallami, *AMIDEAST, Netherlands*

Ammar Al-Hawi, *AMIDEAST, Yemen*

William Albertson, *Drexel University English Language Center, Pennsylvania*

Tara Arntsen, *Northern State University, South Dakota*

Kevin Ballou, *Kobe College, Japan*

Nafisa Bintayeh, *AMIDEAST, Yemen*

Linda Bolet, *Houston Community College, Texas*

Tony Carnerie, *UCSD Extension, English Language Institute, California*

Catherine Cheetham, *Tokai University, Japan*

Celeste Coleman, *CSUSM American Language and Culture Institute, California*

Amy Cook, *Bowling Green State University, Ohio*

Katie Cottier, *University of Texas at Austin, Texas*

Teresita Curbelo, *Instituto Cultural Anglo Uruguayo, Uruguay*

Sarah de Pina, *ELS Boston Downtown, Massachusetts*

Rachel DeSanto, *Hillsborough Community College, Florida*

Silvana Dushku, *Intensive English Institute, Illinois*

Jennie Farnell, *University of Bridgeport, Connecticut*

Rachel Fernandez, *UCI Extension, International Programs, California*

Alayne Flores, *UCSD Extension, English Language Institute, California*

Claire Gimble, *Virginia International University, Virginia*

Floyd H. Graham III, *Kansai Gaidai University, Japan*

Kuei-ping Hsu, *National Tsing Hua University*

James Hughes, *Massachusetts International Academy / UMass Boston, Massachusetts*

Mariano Ignacio, *Centro Universitario de Idiomas, Argentina*

Jules L. Janse van Rensburg, *Chinese Culture University, South Africa*

Rachel Kadish, *GEOS Languages Plus Boston, Massachusetts*

Anthony Lavigne, *Kansai Gaidai University, Japan*

Ai-ping Liu, *National Central University Language Center*

Debra Liu, *City College of San Francisco, California*

Wilder Yesid Escobar Almeciga Imeciga, *Universidad El Bosque, Colombia*

Christina Lorimer, *SDSU American Language Institute, California*

Joanna Luper, *Liberty University, Virginia*

Joy MacFarland, *FLS Boston Commons, Massachusetts*

Elizabeth Mariscal, *UCSD Extension, English Language Institute, California*

Susan McAlister, *Language & Culture Center, University of Houston, Texas*

Wendy McBride, *Spring International Language Center at the University of Arkansas, Arkansas*

Monica McCrory, *University of Texas, Texas*

Katherine Murphy, *Massachusetts International Academy, Massachusetts*

Emily Naber, *Washington English Center, Washington*

Kavitha Nambisan, *University of Tennessee-Martin, Tennessee*

Sandra Navarro, *Glendale Community College, California*

Fernanda Ortiz, *Center for English as a Second Language at the University of Arizona, Arizona*

Pamela Patterson, *Seminole State College, Oklahoma*

Grace Pimcias, *CSUSM American Language and Culture Institute, California*

Jennie Popp, *Universidad Andres Bello, Chile*

Jamie Reinstein, *Community College of Philadelphia, Pennsylvania*

Philip Rice, *University of Delaware, Delaware*

Helen Roland, *Miami Dade College, Florida*

Yoko Sakurai, *Aichi University, Japan*

Jenay Seymour, *Hongik University (Sejong Campus), South Korea*

Margaret Shippey, *Miami Dade College, Florida*

William Slade, *University of Texas at Austin, Texas*

Kelly Smith, *UCSD Extension, English Language Institute, California*

Rachel Stokes, *University of Texas at Austin, Texas*

Joshua Stone, *Approach International Student Center, Massachusetts*

Judy Tanka, *UCLA Extension*

Mary M. Wang, *University of Wisconsin-Madison, Wisconsin*

Judy Wong, *Pace University, New York*

Special thanks to Mary Kadera at TED.

Scope and Sequence

PRONUNCIATION SKILL	NOTE-TAKING SKILL	TED TALKS	PRESENTATION SKILL	UNIT ASSIGNMENT
Use pauses effectively	Use visuals to guide your note taking	*The hidden power of smiling* **Ron Gutman**	Use visuals effectively	Give a group presentation about a habit or activity that has multiple benefits
Stress important Information	Focus on dates and events	*What your doctor won't disclose* **Leana Wen**	Give other people's points of view	Participate in a team debate about the right to privacy vs. the right to know
Intonation for lists	Note the sequence of events	*Want to help someone? Shut up and listen!* **Ernesto Sirolli**	Use gestures	Give a pair presentation about the benefits of listening
Stress in compound nouns	Note causes and effects	*Big data is better data* **Kenneth Cukier**	Follow a clear organization	Give a pair presentation about how big data has helped solve a problem
Thought groups	Use abbreviations for numerical details	*What fear can teach us* **Karen Thompson Walker**	Support your message with a story	Give an individual presentation about how an emotion can teach something useful
Connected speech	Note who says what	*How I fell in love with a fish* **Dan Barber**	Connect with your audience	Role-play an advertisement to promote a sustainable food
Use emphasis for a purpose	Note numbers and their relevance	*The currency of the new economy is trust* **Rachel Botsman**	Include effective supporting details	Present a case study describing a Web site for which the reputation of its users is important
Stress and intonation in comparisons and contrasts	Note key information on slides	*Lies, damned lies, and statistics (about TED Talks)* **Sebastian Wernicke**	Rehearse your talk	Give an individual presentation about a time when you analyzed information to become better at something

Welcome to 21st Century Communication

21st Century Communication: Listening, Speaking, and Critical Thinking develops essential listening, speaking, and presentation skills to help learners succeed with their academic and professional goals. Students learn key academic skills as they engage with thought-provoking TED Talks and 21st century themes and skills, such as global awareness, information literacy, and critical thinking.

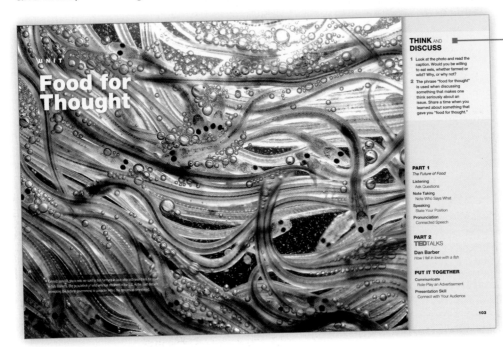

Each unit opens with an impactful photograph related to **a 21st century theme** and Think and Discuss questions to draw students into the topic.

Part 1 introduces a variety of **listening inputs** including lectures, interviews, podcasts, and classroom discussions.

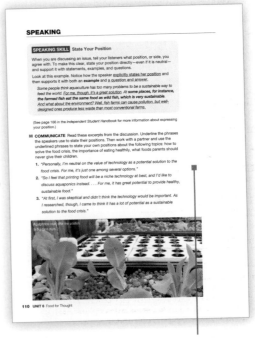

Llistening, speaking, note-taking, and pronunciation skills are explicitly taught and practiced. Woven throughout are 21st century skills of **collaboration, communication,** and **critical thinking**.

How I fell in love
with a fish

" Want to feed the world?
Let's start by asking: How are
we going to feed ourselves? "

BEFORE YOU WATCH

A **COMMUNICATE** Work in a small group. Read the title of the TED Talk and the information about Dan Barber. Then discuss the questions.

1. Barber is described as a "well-known chef." Who are some other well-known chefs? Are they only famous for their cooking abilities?

2. Barber's talk is about falling in love with a fish. What do you think he means by this, and why do you think he chose this title for his talk?

DAN BARBER Chef

Dan Barber is a well-known chef who runs two restaurants in the New York City area. He has won multiple awards for the quality of his cooking. His restaurants serve food that has been grown locally or raised under sustainable conditions. Barber has written books and articles about how delicious food, healthy eating, and sustainable farming should all be connected.

Dan Barber's idea worth spreading is that if we adopt more sustainable food production methods, we can produce food that is good for the planet, good for us, and good to eat.

112 UNIT 6 Food for Thought

Part 2 introduces the TED speaker and the idea worth spreading. Students explore and discuss the ideas while at the same time seamlessly applying the skills learned in Part 1.

Put It Together helps students **connect ideas** and prepares them for their final assignment. Students use a graphic organizer to synthesize information and consolidate their learning.

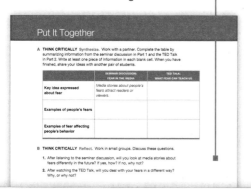

Put It Together

A **THINK CRITICALLY** Synthesize. Work with a partner. Complete the table by summarizing information from the seminar discussion in Part 1 and the TED Talk in Part 2. Write at least one piece of information in each blank cell. When you have finished, share your ideas with another pair of students.

	SEMINAR DISCUSSION: FEAR IN THE MEDIA	TED TALK: WHAT FEAR CAN TEACH US
Key idea expressed about fear	Media stories about people's fears attract readers or viewers.	
Examples of people's fears		
Examples of fear affecting people's behavior		

B **THINK CRITICALLY** Reflect. Work in small groups. Discuss these questions.

1. After listening to the seminar discussion, will you look at media stories about fears differently in the future? If yes, how? If no, why not?

2. After watching the TED Talk, will you deal with your fears in a different way? Why, or why not?

COMMUNICATE

ASSIGNMENT: Role-Play an Advertisement Working in a group, you will create an advertisement and a slogan—a short, memorable phrase used to promote a product or service—for one of these types of sustainable foods. Either act out your advertisement or, if you prefer, present your ideas. Review the ideas in Parts 1 and 2 and the listening and speaking skills as you prepare your presentation on one of these foods:

• Vegetables that have been grown aquaponically
• Meat that has been developed in a laboratory
• Fish that has been farmed at *Veta la Palma*

Infographics engage students more deeply with the unit theme and promote **visual literacy**.

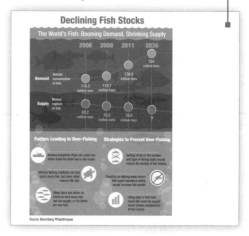

Presentation Skills inspired by the TED speakers give students the skills and authentic language they need to successfully deliver their own presentations.

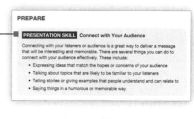

Reflect encourages students to **take charge of their learning**, another 21st century skill.

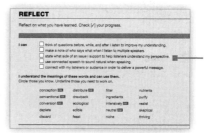

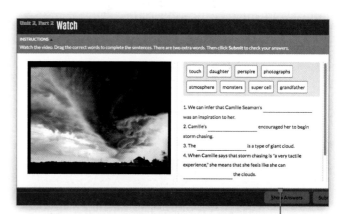

Fully blended **Online Workbooks powered by MyELT** help develop **digital literacy skills** by offering students the complete audio and video program along with speech-recognition and auto-graded language practice activities.

UNIT 1

Free Therapy

Sculptures by artist Yue Minjun add laughter to an outdoor location in Beijing, China.

THINK AND DISCUSS

1 Look at the photo and read the caption. How does looking at these sculptures make you feel? Why?

2 The unit title is part of a longer quote: "Smile, it's free therapy." What do you think this means? In addition to smiling, what else would you describe as "free therapy"?

3

BEFORE YOU LISTEN

A COMMUNICATE Work with a partner. Discuss these questions.

1. Look at the photo. What are some reasons why this person might be outside?

2. You are going to hear a podcast. A podcast is an audio or video file that you subscribe to and access on the Internet. Do you ever listen to podcasts? If yes, what types do you listen to? If no, why not?

3. The podcast you will hear is about improving your life. In your view, is this likely to be a popular topic? Why, or why not?

B 🎧 **1.2** **LISTEN AND INFER** Listen to segment 1 of the podcast by Amanda Forsythe. Then discuss these questions in a small group.

1. Why does Amanda mention buying a new TV?

2. She says that all of her suggestions are based on evidence, are cheap and easy to do, and are ones that she has tried herself. Why do you think she mentions these three things at the start of her podcast?

3. The podcast is about improving your life by taking up simple habits. What are some habits you think she might discuss?

VOCABULARY

C 🎧 **1.3** Read and listen to these sentences with words from the podcast. Guess the meaning of each bold word. Then use one of the bold words to complete each definition below.

a. Stefan was unable to use his computer because its operating system needed a major **upgrade**.

b. After seeing how well his friends did on the test, Ahmed decided to **adopt** the study habits they used.

c. Yuna's parents told her that honesty is a **fundamental** principle in building good relationships.

d. Dan used a few **criteria** when choosing a vacation destination, but his main consideration was cost.

e. Josie made a firm **commitment** to work less and spend more time with her friends and family.

f. Lee's professor advised him to **conduct** an experiment to find out if his theory was accurate.

g. Rachel read that exercising often could lead to better sleep and an **enhanced** overall quality of life.

h. The listeners accepted Bob's ideas because he was able to **cite** research that supported his views.

i. After their baby was born, Deb and Ian had so little sleep they were in a state of constant **fatigue**.

j. Usually Karin could concentrate for hours, but somehow her attention **span** was limited that day.

1. _____ (adj) basic but essential; of central importance

2. _____ (adj) improved or increased

3. _____ (n) a decision or promise to undertake an action

4. _____ (n) an improvement to or new version of something, such as equipment

5. _____ (n) extreme tiredness caused by illness, lack of sleep, or physical effort

6. _____ (n) rules or standards for judging or deciding something

7. _____ (n) the width or length of something, such as a period of time

8. _____ (v) mention or quote information or evidence to support an idea

9. _____ (v) do a particular action, especially research or an experiment

10. _____ (v) start to use or follow something, such as an idea or plan

D COMMUNICATE Discuss these questions with a partner. Use a form of the words in bold in your discussion.

1. What are some things in your life that need an **upgrade?** Why?

2. What are some habits you could **adopt** in order to become better at English?

3. What skills are **fundamental** for success in school? In the workplace?

4. What **criteria** do people tend to use when they buy something big? In your view, which one criterion is the most important?

5. What is one firm **commitment** you have made recently?

6. What is an essential step in **conducting** research?

7. What things typically cause people to feel **fatigue?**

8. At what time of day is your attention **span** typically longest? When is it shortest?

LISTEN

E 🎧 **1.4** ▶ **1.1 LISTEN FOR MAIN IDEAS** Read these summaries, then listen to the podcast. Choose the summary that describes the episode you heard.

AMANDA FORSYTHE: UPGRADE YOUR LIFE – AVAILABLE EPISODES			
1	**Eat Your Way to Weight Loss** Too good to be true? Limit what you eat twice a week, eat what you want on other days, and still lose weight.	▶	⬇ 👍
2	**Daily Steps to Better Health** Got a free half hour? Discover the physical and mental benefits of going for a daily walk, especially outside.	▶	⬇ 👍
3	**Time to Take a Stand** Are you a couch potato? You can improve your health by spending less time sitting and more time standing.	▶	⬇ 👍

WORDS IN THE PODCAST
cardiac (adj): related to the heart, especially when discussing medical issues
depression (n): a mental illness with symptoms that include feeling unhappy and lacking energy
diabetes (n): a disease that causes the body to have too much sugar (in the form of glucose)

F 🎧 **1.5** **LISTEN FOR DETAILS** Listen to segment 2 of the podcast and complete these profiles with details.

Name   Mike Evans

Nationality   Canadian

Roles   _____
                                     1

               Associate professor

               _____ broadcaster
                            2

Idea   Walk for _____
                                      3
               minutes daily

Name   David Suzuki

Nationality   _____
                                     4

Roles   _____
                                     5

               Academic

               Environmental activist

Idea   Spend time in

               _____
                                     6

LISTENING SKILL **Listen for Supporting Evidence**

Speakers often support their ideas, theories, or opinions with evidence. This can involve summarizing research studies. Supporting evidence is important, so you should listen carefully and take detailed notes when a speaker provides evidence. Generally, speakers will mention some or all of the following details:

- Who did the research and/or where it was conducted (e.g., a university or region)
- When and/or for how long it took place
- What the results of the research were

G 🎧 **1.6** Listen to segment 3 of the podcast. Fill in the supporting evidence in these notes.

Study from _____ in _____
                        1   2

⇝ walking to work = _____
                                  3

Study of _____ conducted by prof at Arnold
                        4

School of _____ Health at U of S Carolina
                        5

⇝ lower fitness level = _____
                                    6

H **COMMUNICATE** Work with a partner. Answer these questions about the notes in exercise G.

1. In addition to the studies summarized in exercise G, what other support does the speaker give for her idea that walking every day is beneficial?

2. What abbreviations (short ways to write something) are used in the notes? What do they stand for?

3. Which other words in the notes could be abbreviated? How would you abbreviate them?

4. What symbols and abbreviations do you typically use when you take notes?

AFTER YOU LISTEN

I **COMMUNICATE** Work in a small group. Discuss these questions.

1. After listening to the podcast, are you motived to walk every day for 30 minutes and/or spend more time in nature? Why, or why not?

2. The speaker doesn't give information about her background, but cites several experts and studies. Whose advice are you more likely to listen to, a person you know or an expert? Explain.

3. Look again at exercise E on page 6. Would you be interested in listening to podcasts 1 and 3? Why, or why not?

4. If you had to give a podcast about how to upgrade your life, what would you choose to talk about?

SPEAKING

J Complete this quiz to determine if your life could benefit from an upgrade.

Should You Upgrade Your Life?

Each day (or night) on average, how many . . .	
1. hours do you sleep?	6
2. glasses of water do you drink?	9
3. times do you eat vegetables or a piece of fruit?	2
4. times do you feel grateful to somebody or for something?	1
Each week on average, how many times do you . . .	
5. use floss (thin string) to clean between your teeth?	0
6. do something with your friends?	2
7. do some physical activity, such as walking or running?	4
8. do some mental activity, such as a crossword or Sudoku puzzle?	7
Total	31

Scoring

Up to 25 points—You might want to think seriously about upgrading your life.

Up to 35 points—Are there one or two areas of your life you could upgrade?

Over 35 points—Your life seems to be in pretty good shape—keep it up!

K **THINK CRITICALLY** Interpret Results. Work in a small group. Calculate and then discuss your scores. If you want to upgrade some aspects of your life, what will you upgrade first? Why?

SPEAKING SKILL Emphasize Key Details

To help listeners recognize and understand key details, it's a good idea to emphasize them. There are several ways you can do this:

1. Speak more slowly and clearly each time you mention a key detail. You can pronounce it with emphasis, too.

2. Pause slightly before and after you mention a key detail, especially the first time.

3. Mention the key detail more than once.

4. If the key detail is a name, spell it out—for example: "Uppsala . . . that's U—double P—S—A—L—A."

L COMMUNICATE Work with a partner. Discuss these questions.

1. Which of the suggestions for emphasizing key details mentioned in the skills box would be easiest for you to adopt? Why?

2. The skills box says that names can be key details. What other kinds of information can be key details? (Look at exercise F on page 7 for ideas if necessary.)

PRONUNCIATION SKILL Use Pauses Effectively

Speakers often worry about having too much silence when they give a talk or speech, but appropriate pausing is an important aspect of effective, clear speech. In most cases, pauses between words, ideas, and sentences should be short. In some situations, however, it can be effective to pause for a longer time—up to several seconds. Reasons for pausing for a longer time include the following:

1. To allow listeners to study a visual you are using to illustrate your talk

2. To give listeners time to understand a long and/or complex idea you have just mentioned

3. To signify that you are about to move on to a new point or the next part of your talk

4. To build tension and interest among listeners about what you are going to say next

M 🎧 **1.7** Listen to segment 4, which includes three short excerpts from the podcast. Why does the speaker use a long pause in each excerpt?

1. In excerpt 1, the long pause . . .
   a. signifies that the speaker is moving on to a new point or part of her talk.
   b. builds tension and interest in what the speaker is going to say next.

2. In excerpt 2, the long pause . . .
   a. gives listeners time to understand a long and/or complex idea.
   b. signifies that the speaker is moving on to a new point or part of her talk.

3. In excerpt 3, the long pause . . .
   a. gives listeners time to understand a long and/or complex idea.
   b. builds tension and interest in what the speaker is going to say next.

Millennium Park is a popular place for people to hang out, see films, or listen to music in Chicago, Illinois, U.S.

N Choose one of these suggested topics to talk about for 60 seconds. Make some notes about your chosen topic. Mark on the notes where you will use long pauses and decide what information you will emphasize to help your listeners understand the key details in your talk.

Topic 1: A place you know well

- Say what this place is called.
- Say where this place is located.
- Describe some interesting things you can do in this place.

Topic 2: A good friend

- Say your friend's full name.
- Say where and when you met this person.
- Describe some of this person's good qualities.

Topic 3: A TV program you enjoy

- Say what this program is called.
- Name the main characters in the program.
- Give some reasons why you like watching this program.

O **COMMUNICATE** Work in a small group. Take turns giving a 60-second talk about your topic. After each talk, discuss whether it was easy to hear the key details or not. Also discuss how effectively the speaker used pauses.

The hidden
power of
smiling

" Whenever you want to tap into
a superpower that will help you and
everyone around you live a longer,
healthier, happier life, smile. **"**

BEFORE YOU WATCH

A COMMUNICATE Read the title of the TED Talk and the information about Ron
Gutman. What is an entrepreneur? Do you find it surprising that an entrepreneur
would be interested in helping people live longer and healthier lives? Why, or why
not? Discuss in small groups.

> **RON GUTMAN** Entrepreneur
>
> Since he was a graduate student, Ron Gutman has been interested in helping
> people lead healthier, happier lives. He has founded and run several companies.
> His current business, HealthTap, provides reliable and free health information.
> Gutman also advises and invests in other health and technology companies.
>
> Ron Gutman's idea worth spreading is that smiling—one of the most basic,
> universal human expressions—actually helps us live longer and healthier lives.

B COMMUNICATE Work in a small group. Discuss these questions. When you have
finished, share your ideas with the class.

1. Are you surprised by the effects Gutman claims smiling has? Why, or why not?

2. Things that improve our health have either a physical or mental effect on us. In your
view, which effect or effects does smiling probably have? Support your opinion.

VOCABULARY

C 🎧 **1.8** These definitions will help you learn words in the TED Talk. Add one of the bold words to each blank to complete the sentences below. Use the correct form for verbs. Then listen to the sentences to check your answers.

- **a. well-being** (n) a person's physical and mental condition
- **b. fulfilling** (adj) causing happiness and satisfaction as a result of doing something
- **c. initially** (adv) at first, or existing or happening at the beginning of something
- **d. renowned** (adj) widely known, especially for a positive quality
- **e. mimic** (v) copy something, especially a person's actions, words, or manner of speaking
- **f. determine** (v) decide, especially by researching or thinking about something
- **g. stimulate** (v) perform an action to encourage something to happen
- **h. modify** (v) change or alter something
- **i. competent** (adj) having the ability or skills to do something well
- **j. frown** (v) look disapproving, angry, or doubtful

1. Scholars _____ thought there were only two types of smiles: real and fake. But recent research conducted by _____ psychologist Paul Ekman suggests there are actually 18 different kinds.

2. Studies suggest that people who _____ often are rated as less attractive than those who smile often. Such people may also be considered less _____, or skilled, at their jobs than they really are.

3. Surveys show that those who often smile at work find their jobs more emotionally _____ than people who smile less often at work. The surveys further suggest that smiling regularly at work can improve people's overall sense of job satisfaction and their _____.

4. When babies _____ the sounds they hear and copy the facial expressions they see, they are actually learning how to communicate. As a result, adults can _____ communicative ability in infants by using a variety of facial expressions when speaking to them.

5. When faced with an unproven theory, academics undertake research studies to _____ whether or not it is correct. If the results show that the theory is wrong or incomplete, scholars may _____ it or come up with a new theory.

D COMMUNICATE Discuss these questions with a partner. Use one or more forms of the bold word when you answer each question.

1. In your opinion, what things contribute most to people's **well-being**?

2. Think of a time when you **modified** your opinion about something. What did you **initially** think, and how and why did your opinion change?

3. Think of a **renowned** person in your country. Why is he or she well known?

4. Is it generally positive or negative to **mimic** another person? Support your view.

5. From your perspective, what skills or qualities make a person appear **competent**?

6. What are some other reasons to avoid **frowning**, aside from the ones mentioned in exercise C?

WATCH

learn**more** A superhero is a fictional character with special powers. Superheroes appear in comic books or fantasy or science fiction stories. Superman is an example of a superhero. According to the stories, he made an intergalactic journey—across the galaxy—to Earth from a planet called Krypton. His powers include super strength and the ability to fly.

E ▶ 1.2 WATCH FOR MAIN IDEAS Watch the TED Talk and notice how Gutman organizes his ideas. Then number each summary statement (1–5) to show the order in which he covers each point.

_3_   He describes additional scientific experiments on smiling.

_1_   He gives an introduction to himself and his research.

_4_   He compares smiling with other things that make us feel good.

_2_   He explains that smiling is a basic, universal human expression.

_5_   He sums up some of the benefits of smiling he has already mentioned.

WORDS IN THE TALK

contagious (adj): describing a disease or emotion that easily spreads from person to person
courteous (adj): polite, well-mannered
facial (adj): related to or affecting the face
hormones (n): natural body chemicals that influence behavior and feelings
25 grand (n): (informal) 25,000 dollars (or other currency)

NOTE-TAKING SKILL Use Visuals to Guide Your Note Taking

Speakers sometimes use visuals when they deliver a presentation or lecture. Often, when the visual changes, the speaker is about to make a new and important point. This means you can use the visuals as a guide for what to take notes about and when to start a new point in your notes. Sometimes the visual will show information that the speaker does not say, so you should be prepared to take notes about what you see as well as what you hear.

F ▶ **1.3** **WATCH FOR DETAILS** Watch segment 1 of the TED Talk. Take notes when the visual changes. Then use your notes to write short answers to these questions.

1. In what year was the research study at Wayne State University conducted?

_____

2. The researchers looked at baseball cards from before which decade?

_____

3. On average, how long did players who didn't smile live?

_____

4. How long did players with wide, beaming smiles live on average?

_____

5. What do blind babies do when they hear the sound of a human voice?

_____

G ▶ **1.4** **WATCH FOR SUPPORTING EVIDENCE** Read the statements. Then watch segment 2 of the TED Talk. Match the supporting studies that Gutman mentions to the correct research finding.

1. **B** ___ A recent study conducted at Uppsala University in Sweden

2. **E** ___ A recent study from the University of Clermont-Ferrand in France

3. **A** ___ An experiment conducted by French neurologist Guillaume Duchenne

4. **D** ___ A German study that used fMRI imaging to measure brain activity

5. **C** ___ A study undertaken by researchers in Britain

6. **F** ___ A recent study conducted at Penn State University in the U.S.

a. It is possible to stimulate somebody to smile by sending electricity to his or her facial muscles.

b. It's difficult to frown when you are looking at a smiling person because smiling is contagious.

c. One smile generates the same level of brain stimulation as receiving a lot of money or chocolate.

d. Smiling modifies how our brains process emotions so that we actually feel better when we smile.

e. Subjects who held a pencil in their mouths found it difficult to determine if a smile was real or fake.

f. When we smile, other people feel that we look more likeable, courteous, and competent.

H ▶ **1.5** **EXPAND YOUR VOCABULARY** Watch the excerpts from the TED Talk. Guess the meanings of the phrases in the box.

> long-lasting   stumble upon   aha! moment
> impaired judgment   tap into

AFTER YOU WATCH

| **THINK CRITICALLY** Interpret an Infographic. Work with a partner. The infographic lists the benefits of smiling. Categorize the benefits by writing the number of each one in the chart below. Some may fit in more than one category. Put a check (✓) next to the benefits that Gutman mentions.

Source: 1st Family Dental

EFFECTS ON YOUR BODY	**EFFECTS ON YOUR MOOD**	**EFFECTS ON OTHER PEOPLE**	**OTHER EFFECTS**
1 3 7 10	1 8 2 9 3 10 4 6	1 8 2 9 3 4 6	1 5 8 9 10

Pickles

J **COLLABORATE** Interview five students in your class to find out what their top three reasons for smiling are. They may choose from the reasons in the infographic or come up with their own.

STUDENT'S NAME	REASON #1	REASON #2	REASON #3

K **THINK CRITICALLY** **Interpret Results.** Work in a small group. Discuss these questions.

1. What are the most and least common reasons why people in your class smile?

2. Why do you think these reasons are the most and least common?

3. Do you think you would get the same results if you interviewed a group of school children or a group of business leaders? Why, or why not?

Put It Together

A **THINK CRITICALLY** Synthesize. Work in a small group. Discuss these questions.

1. In Part 1, you listened to a podcast about how people can upgrade their lives. Do you think the speaker would consider smiling more to be a life upgrade? Why, or why not?

2. In the TED Talk in Part 2, Ron Gutman argues that smiling is a "superpower" that has many positive effects. Do you think he would agree that walking every day is also a superpower? Why, or why not?

COMMUNICATE

ASSIGNMENT: Give a Group Presentation You will give a group presentation about a simple habit or activity that has multiple physical, emotional, or other benefits—something that upgrades your life. Ideas for possible topics include:

- Eat a rainbow of colored foods, especially fruits and vegetables, at every meal.
- Get a pet or spend more time with your friends in order to reduce your stress levels.
- Watch TED Talks to learn some ideas worth spreading and then adopt some of the ideas.

PREPARE

B Work in a small group. Create an outline of your presentation. Use these questions as a guide.

- What habit or activity will you discuss?
- How and where should people do it?
- When and how often should people do it?
- What are the benefits of doing it?
- What evidence supports these benefits?

PRESENTATION SKILL Use Visuals Effectively

Using visuals is a great way to make a presentation more interesting and memorable. Here are some strategies for choosing suitable visuals and for using visuals effectively:

- Choose images that are bright, clear, and relevant, but do not use too many of them.

- If you include words on a slide, focus on just two or three key points written in simple phrases.

- Don't distract your audience with too many animated images or special visual effects.

- The visuals are for your audience, not you; don't turn away from the audience to look at your visuals.

- After you show an image, pause in order to give your audience time to study it.

- Give the source for your images – either on the slide or verbally.

C ▶ 1.6 **COLLABORATE** Work in your presentation group. Watch an excerpt from the TED Talk. Then discuss these questions.

1. What do you find most effective about Gutman's use of images?

2. Review your presentation outline from exercise B. Where could you use visuals? Find some interesting images to support the points you will make.

D **COLLABORATE** Work in your presentation group. Decide who will answer each question in your outline. Then practice delivering your presentation until you feel confident. Help each other to deliver the presentation well. Focus on:

- Supporting your points with evidence

- Emphasizing key details

- Using pauses effectively

- Using visuals effectively

E Read the rubric on page 179. Notice how your presentation will be evaluated. Keep these categories in mind as you present and watch your classmates' presentations.

PRESENT

F Give your group presentation to the class. Watch other groups' presentations. After you watch each one, provide feedback using the rubric as a guide. Add notes or any other feedback you want to share.

G **THINK CRITICALLY** **Evaluate.** Work in a small group. Make sure that each member of your group delivered a different presentation. Share feedback on the presentations you watched and listen to feedback about your group's presentation. Then discuss these questions.

1. What aspect of your group's presentation were you most satisfied with?

2. What aspect of your group's presentation were you least satisfied with?

3. What did you learn from watching presentations by the other groups?

REFLECT

Reflect on what you have learned. Check [✓] your progress.

I can
- [ ] listen for supporting evidence, such as research studies.
- [ ] emphasize key details when I speak.
- [ ] use pauses effectively.
- [ ] use visuals to guide my note taking.
- [ ] use visuals effectively in my presentations.

I understand the meanings of these words and can use them.
Circle those you know. Underline those you need to work on.

adopt	criteria AWL	fulfilling	renowned
cite AWL	determine	fundamental AWL	span
commitment AWL	enhance AWL	initially AWL	stimulate
competent	fatigue	mimic	upgrade
conduct AWL	frown	modify AWL	well-being

UNIT 2
The Right to Know

Siblings Julie, Antonio, and India Abram from Flint, Michigan, collect their daily allowance of bottled water. In 2015, the people in Flint learned that their water supply had been contaminated by lead, causing a public health emergency.

THINK AND DISCUSS

1 Look at the photo and read the caption. How do you think this experience might impact the children in positive ways?

2 People should have the right to know if their water supply is polluted. What other things should people have the right to know?

PART 1
Moving Society Forward

Note Taking
Focus on Dates and Events

Listening
Listen for Multiple Viewpoints

Speaking
Use Figurative Language

Pronunciation
Stress Important Information

PART 2
TEDTALKS

Leana Wen
What your doctor won't disclose

PUT IT TOGETHER

Communicate
Participate in a Team Debate

Presentation Skill
Give Other People's Points of View

23

BEFORE YOU LISTEN

Women circa 1912 marched in New York for the right to vote

A COMMUNICATE Work with a partner. Discuss these questions.

1. Look at the photo. How does it represent a move forward in society?

2. What are some positive social movements that have happened recently?

3. What is one positive social movement that you would like to see happen in the future? Why?

B 🎧 **1.9** Listen to segment 1 of an academic lecture. According to the professor, what will the class focus on?

    a. how societies develop into formal or informal groups

    b. what social movements are and what their purpose is

    c. why societies rarely change in positive ways

VOCABULARY

C 🎧 **1.10** Read and listen to these sentences with words from the lecture. Then choose the answer that is closest in meaning to the bold word.

1. The government's plan to make citizens with high earnings pay more taxes is **controversial**.
   a. causing public disagreement   **b.** generating a lot of amusement   **c.** becoming more uncertain

2. **Institutions** such as banks, hospitals, and universities, play a vital role in modern society.
   a. popular places to visit   **b.** innovative places to work   **c.** important organizations

3. The manager's policy was to be **transparent** and explain in detail why she made each decision.
   a. open and obvious   **b.** friendly but careful   **c.** strong and professional

4. The magazine article **disclosed** details about the politician's career that few people knew.
   a. learned   **b.** opened   **c.** shared

5. The company paid back the employee's hotel and travel **expenses** after his business trip to China.
   a. costs that vary frequently   **b.** work costs that are repaid   **c.** prices of things overseas

6. The **revelation** that the company was releasing a new smartphone caused its stock price to rise.
   a. uncertain event   **b.** important decision   **c.** unexpected information

7. Sales of the product **collapsed** when a competitor introduced a similar, but much cheaper, product.
   a. failed suddenly   **b.** declined slowly   **c.** ended eventually

8. The **investigation** found previously unknown evidence, and the police quickly solved the case.
   a. discussion about a situation   **b.** review of known facts   **c.** search for new information

9. The government launched a new employment **initiative** to help unemployed citizens find jobs.
   a. strong argument   **b.** positive action   **c.** popular location

10. The CEO was surprised by the survey that showed many consumers felt **mistrust** for the brand.
    a. danger or fear   **b.** dislike or irritation   **c.** suspicion or doubt

D **COMMUNICATE** Discuss these questions with a partner. Use a form of the bold word when you answer each question.

1. In your view, does the media just *report on* **controversial** stories, or does it also *contribute to* them? Explain your answer.

2. Which **institutions** do you feel are more important for society: banks, hospitals, or universities? Why?

3. What are some advantages and disadvantages of being **transparent** at work? With friends?

4. What kinds of information about famous people might magazine articles **disclose?**

5. Give an example of a surprising **revelation** you have had or have read about. Why was it surprising?

6. If consumers feel **mistrust** for a company, how can that company regain consumers' trust?

LISTEN

E 🎧 **1.11** ▶ **1.7** **LISTEN FOR MAIN IDEAS** Listen to the lecture. Check (✓) the three answers that summarize the main points that the professor makes.

1. _____ Politicians around the world are unfamiliar with social movements such as the right to know movement.

2. ✓ The right to know movement focuses on getting organizations to disclose information.

3. ✓ The movement for transparency aims to get organizations to be open with information.

4. _____ The global financial crisis of 2008 was mainly the result of organizations not acting transparently.

5. ✓ The right to know and transparency movements led to political changes in the U.K. and Iceland.

NOTE-TAKING SKILL Focus on Dates and Events

Dates are usually important details in a talk or lecture. If a speaker mentions a date, such as a year, decade, or century, note both the date and the event that happened. Save time by using abbreviations for both dates and events.

Examples:	**Speaker Says**	**Notes**
	Profits declined from 1970 to 1979.	profits ↓ in 70s
	Governments shared more information in the twentieth century.	Govts shared ↑ info in 20C

The country of Iceland was the most affected by the global financial crisis of 2008.

F 🎧 **1.12 LISTEN FOR DETAILS** Listen to segment 2, which includes four excerpts from the lecture. Complete these notes by adding the dates and events you hear.

1. Right to know movem—began in _____ after

_____ by R Carson

2. In _____ journalist H Brooke

_____ about politicians in UK

3. Finan. crisis affected Iceland in _____ → three main banks

_____ & value of _____

4. Business survey from _____ =

_____ mistrust companies

LISTENING SKILL Listen for Multiple Viewpoints

Some speakers support their view with the ideas of other people or organizations. This adds to the credibility of their view. Speakers may also include opposing viewpoints to present both sides of an issue or to argue against the opposing view. By listening for multiple viewpoints, you will better understand not only the speaker's ideas but also other opinions about the same topic. Notice how the speaker introduces an opposing view with the word *however*.

"In my view, governments should be more transparent. In a survey from 2015, more than 60 percent of Americans expressed the same view. However, some worry that transparency could be expensive to introduce."

G 🎧 **1.13** Listen to segment 3, which includes excerpts from the lecture. Whose point(s) of view does the professor discuss in each excerpt? Write the excerpt number (1-4) next to the viewpoint(s). Two excerpts match two viewpoints.

_____ Environmentally-concerned citizens

_____ McDonald's Canada

_____ North American consumers

_____ Politicians in Iceland

_____ Residents of the U.K.

_____ The people of Iceland

AFTER YOU LISTEN

H THINK CRITICALLY Evaluate. Work with a partner. In the lecture, the professor gives three examples of positive changes in society. In your view, which example had the biggest impact on a society? Why?

1. The change in how politicians in the U.K. can claim expenses

2. The demand for political transparency from citizens in Iceland

3. The way that McDonald's Canada is being open with customers

I COLLABORATE Interview other students to complete this survey.

The professor says McDonald's Canada will answer questions that consumers post on a Web site. Interview other students to complete this survey.

What Would You Ask?

If you could question any company, which company would you choose and what question would you ask?

STUDENT'S NAME	COMPANY	QUESTION

J COMMUNICATE Work with a partner. Take turns following these steps.

- Tell your partner the name of one student you interviewed and the question he or she would ask.

- Ask your partner to guess the company that the student would like to ask this question to.

SPEAKING

SPEAKING SKILL Use Figurative Language

Speakers sometimes use figurative language. This kind of language describes a thing or an idea as being like something else. It can make a speaker's words and ideas more interesting and convincing. Three common types of figurative language are:

1. *Simile*—directly comparing two things with an explicit connecting word such as *like, as,* or *than:*
   The *rain clouds* were *as black as night.*

2. *Metaphor*—indirectly comparing two things without the use of an explicit connecting word:
   He had *a stormy relationship* with his father.

3. *Personification*—using human characteristics or actions to describe something not human:
   They listened to *the wind singing* in the trees.

K COMMUNICATE Work with a partner. Look at three examples of figurative language from the lecture. Write the type of figurative language the speaker uses in each. Then discuss the best answer to each question.

1. *"To sum up, right to know focuses on what people want organizations to disclose. Transparency is about what organizations choose to disclose. As I said, they're like opposite sides of the same coin."*

   By using the _____ "like opposites sides of the same coin," the speaker is suggesting that

   a. right to know and transparency are both valuable ideas.

   b. right to know and transparency are different but connected.

2. *"The highest U.K. court ruled that citizens had the right to know and shouldn't be kept in the dark."*

   By using the _____ "kept in the dark," the speaker is suggesting that

   a. disclosing information is like turning on a light.

   b. citizens were angry until they had the right to know.

3. *"This transparency initiative . . . [is] a step in the right direction."*

   By using the _____ of the transparency initiative being "a step in the right direction," the speaker is

   a. pointing out that the situation is likely to improve very slowly.

   b. suggesting that the situation is likely to continue getting better.

L COLLABORATE Work in a small group. Read this excerpt from the lecture. Then come up with figurative language to express some of the ideas in the excerpt. When you have finished, share your ideas with the class.

> *"Another example is the case of the global financial crisis of 2008. Iceland was affected by this crisis more than any other country. Its three main banks collapsed. The value of its currency fell by half. The stock market lost more than 90 percent of its value. And levels of inflation and foreign debt rose dramatically."*

A: *Iceland was "hurt" or "sickened" by this crisis.*

B: *That's a good way of putting it.*

PRONUNCIATION SKILL Stress Important Information

Every sentence has several words that relay the most important information. Speakers use stress to make sure the listener focuses on these words. They may say the important information more loudly, clearly, and with a higher pitch than the rest of the sentence. They may say new or unfamiliar words more slowly and pause after saying them. Important information may include:

⌓ **1.14**

Main ideas or key concepts:

*To sum up, **right to know** focuses on what people want **organizations** to **disclose**. **Transparency** is about what **organizations choose** to **disclose**.*

Numbers, dates, and names:

*Back in **2004**, a journalist named **Heather Brooke** began requesting information.*

Negative words:

*The highest U.K. court ruled that citizens had the right to know and **shouldn't** be kept in the dark.*

M ⌓ 1.15 Work in a small group. Listen to segment 4 of the lecture. What information does the speaker stress? Why do you think he stresses these words?

N COLLABORATE Work with a partner. Choose one of these situations and discuss it. Then present your ideas to the class: one of you should present the advantages, and the other should present the disadvantages. When you present, focus on stressing important information and use figurative language, if possible.

Discuss the advantages and disadvantages of ONE of these situations:

- Parents being transparent about their decisions when they speak to their children
- Politicians being transparent about their policies when they communicate with voters
- Teachers being transparent about their teaching methods when they talk to their students
- Companies being transparent about their profits when they communicate with their customers
- Doctors being transparent about their training and experience when they speak to their patients

What your doctor won't disclose

TEDMED

" People want to know about their doctors. **"**

BEFORE YOU WATCH

A COMMUNICATE Work in a small group. Discuss these questions.

1. Read the information about Leana Wen. In what ways does she sound like a good doctor?

2. Read the title of the TED Talk and the quote. What do you think people want to know about their doctors that their doctors don't tell them?

LEANA WEN Doctor and Public Health Advocate

Dr. Leana Wen was born in China. She moved to the U.S. as a child and began training to become a doctor while still a teenager. She has worked at Harvard Medical School, done research at the World Health Organization, and written a book to improve communication between patients and doctors. She currently works as Commissioner at the Baltimore City Health Department and as Director of Patient-Centered Care Research in the Department of Emergency Medicine at George Washington University. Her professional goal and personal mission is to practice patient-centered care that is 0% fear and 100% trust.

Leana Wen's idea worth spreading is that doctors should build trust with their patients through "total transparency," which means sharing their personal values as well as any conflicts of interest they might have.

B COMMUNICATE Work in a small group. Read this definition. Then discuss the questions below.

A **conflict of interest** occurs when a person (or an organization) has multiple interests, one of which could affect the judgment behind his or her decisions and actions. For example, it would be a conflict of interest for a journalist to write a story promoting a business that he or she owns.

1. In her TED Talk, Wen says her mother's doctor was a highly paid speaker for a drug company. Why could this be a conflict of interest for him?

2. Wen thinks doctors should disclose possible conflicts of interests to their patients. Do you agree that doctors should do this? Why, or why not?

3. Some doctors might disagree with Wen's view. What reasons do you think they might have?

VOCABULARY

C 🎧 **1.16** These sentences will help you learn words in the TED Talk. Read and listen to the sentences. Then choose one word from each sentence to complete the definitions.

a. The student **pursued** her goal of becoming a doctor by focusing on her studies and working hard.

b. The man was pleased to learn that his doctor was not acting **on behalf of** any drug companies.

c. The patient's problem disappeared after her doctor **prescribed** the right medicine for her.

d. The **respondent** gave very detailed and helpful answers to the questions in the health survey.

e. The internist, or doctor specializing in treating adults, had a close **affiliation** with a charitable organization as well as a relationship with several local clinics.

f. The patients received a small sum of money as an **incentive** for taking part in the medical trial.

g. The doctor was interested in bone disorders, so she chose orthopedics as her medical **specialty**.

h. The man was **ashamed of** being unfit and felt guilty for not taking his doctor's advice to exercise.

i. The woman qualified as a **physician** after completing eleven years of medical school and training.

j. The patient's weakness made him **vulnerable** to infection, so the surgeon canceled the operation.

1. **pursue** (v) work hard (often over a long period of time) in order to achieve a _____*goal*_____

2. **on behalf of** (prep) _____ as a representative of an organization or person

3. **prescribe** (v) write an order for _____ or suggest an action that might be helpful

4. **respondent** (n) a person who responds to the questions in a _____ or questionnaire

5. **affiliation** (n) an official _____ or connection between a person and an organization

6. **incentive** (n) a reward, such as _____, for doing something or working for somebody

7. **specialty** (n) a job or subject that a person, such as a _____, has expert knowledge about

8. **ashamed of** (adj) feeling _____ or embarrassed about one's actions or characteristics

9. **physician** (n) a person with _____ training who is qualified to work as a doctor

10. **vulnerable** (adj) likely to become sick or be hurt because of _____ or lack of protection

D COMMUNICATE Discuss these questions with a partner. Use one or more forms of the bold words when you answer each question.

1. Would you agree that the act of **pursuing** a goal or dream is more beneficial than actually achieving it? Why, or why not?

2. In general, what kinds of people act **on behalf of** other people? Is this something you would be comfortable doing? Why, or why not?

3. When some people see a doctor, they only feel satisfied if he or she gives them a **prescription** for some medicine. Do you feel this way? Why, or why not?

4. In your view, what are the most powerful **incentives** that motivate people to take some kind of action?

5. The writer Alexander Pope once said, "No one should be **ashamed** to admit they are wrong." Do you agree with his words? Why, or why not?

6. If you could choose only one of these three careers, would you rather be a lawyer, a politician, or a **physician?** Why?

WATCH

learnmore In her TED Talk, Leana Wen mentions the Sunshine Act. The full name of this law, passed by the U.S. government in 2010 to improve patient safety, is the Physicia Payments Sunshine Act. Under this law, businesses that mak medical supplies must be transparent about payments they make to doctors or nurses. For example, if a company that s chemotherapy drugs to treat cancer has a financial relationsh with an oncologist, a doctor whose specialty is treating cancer, it must disclose this to a government agency.

E ▶ **1.8** **WATCH FOR MAIN IDEAS** Read these quotes from Wen's talk. Then watch the edited TED Talk. Number the quotes in the order you hear them. Finally, work in a small group and discuss which four of the quotes illustrate Wen's main ideas.

__6__ "Being totally transparent is scary. You feel naked, exposed, and vulnerable, but that vulnerability, that humility, it can be an extraordinary benefit to the practice of medicine."

__4__ "People want to know about their doctors first so that they can make an informed choice. As a result of this, I formed a campaign, Who's My Doctor?, that calls for total transparency in medicine."

__5__ "Research has shown us that openness also helps doctors, that having open medical records, being willing to talk about medical errors, will increase patient trust."

__3__ "Suhavi Tucker and Laura Johns literally took their research to the streets. They went to banks, coffee shops, senior centers, Chinese restaurants, and train stations."

__2__ "When it comes to medicine, having that trust is a must, and when that trust is gone, then all that's left is fear."

__1__ "Well, we all have that childhood hero that we want to grow up to be just like, right? Well, I wanted to be just like Dr. Sam."

WORDS IN THE TALK

asthma (n): a health condition that makes it hard to breathe
backlash (n): a strong, negative reaction by many people against somebody or something
malpractice (n): a wrong (or illegal) action by a doctor or lawyer that causes harm to a patient or client
traitor (n): a person who is not loyal to their country, organization, or group

F ▶ **1.9** **WATCH FOR DETAILS** Read the information about Wen's *Who's My Doctor?* campaign for transparency in medicine. Choose the best word from the box to complete each sentence. One word won't be used. Then watch segment 1 of the edited TED Talk and check your answers.

> huge   medical   public   surprising   total   voluntary

Leana Wen's campaign calls for _____ transparency in
                                                    1

medicine. Participating doctors can disclose information such as where they did their

_____ training. They can also disclose their specialty, conflicts
                  2

of interest, and how they get paid. The information that doctors choose to disclose is posted

on a _____ Web site. Doctors do not need to participate in the
                  3

campaign because it is entirely _____ . Despite this, there was a
                                                    4

_____ backlash from some doctors when the campaign began.
                  5

G ▶ **1.8** **WATCH FOR MULTIPLE VIEWPOINTS** Watch the edited TED Talk again. Match the viewpoints to the groups of people. Two viewpoints match one group.

1. _____ One or both of Leana Wen's parents

2. _____ Respondents in Wen's research study

3. _____ Doctors who are against Wen's campaign

4. _____ Patients who want doctors to be transparent

5. _____ Physicians participating in Wen's campaign

a. I don't want to tell my patients my income because they don't tell me the same information.

b. I feel being a transparent doctor has helped me develop a better relationship with patients.

c. I hope that my doctor uses science and evidence as the basis for his or her decisions.

d. I think doctors should disclose conflicts of interest since lawyers and politicians must also do this.

e. I want to know about my doctor's values because my relationship with my doctor should be close.

f. I worry that my doctor prescribed medicine that benefits him financially but may not benefit me.

Wen's medical students conducted their research in Chinese restaurants, coffee shops, and senior centers.

H INTERPRET FIGURATIVE LANGUAGE Work with a partner. Read this excerpt from Wen's TED Talk. Then discuss your answers to the questions.

"Doctors are scared, too. We're scared of patients finding out who we are and what medicine is all about. And so, what do we do? We put on our white coats and we hide behind them. Of course, the more we hide, the more people want to know what it is that we're hiding. The more fear then spirals into mistrust and poor medical care. Can we bridge this disconnect between what patients need and what doctors do? Can we overcome the sickness of fear?"

1. What does Wen mean when she says, "We put on our white coats and we hide behind them"?
   a. White coats separate doctors from patients as they represent the authority that doctors have.
   b. Doctors believe that their white coats will limit the number of questions that patients ask.

2. What does Wen mean when she says, "Fear then spirals into mistrust and poor medical care"?
   a. Fear and mistrust are more often caused by poor medical care than by other factors.
   b. Fear leads to mistrust which leads to poor medical care which leads back to more fear.

3. What does Wen mean when she asks, "Can we bridge this disconnect?"
   a. Can we discover a way to connect two or more unrelated things?
   b. Can we build a link to join things that are currently separated?

4. What does Wen mean when she refers to a "sickness of fear"?
   a. Fear can spread and affect other people.
   b. Fear can cause people to feel physically ill.

I ▶ **1.10 EXPAND YOUR VOCABULARY** Watch the excerpts from the TED Talk. Guess the meanings of the phrases in the box.

provoke anger	take an oath	short of breath
deeply intimate	ensue	change the paradigm

J WATCH MORE Go to TED.com to watch the full TED talk by Leana Wen.

AFTER YOU WATCH

K THINK CRITICALLY Interpret an Infographic. Work with a partner. Write in the quality that matches each description in the infographic.

accessible   competent   reliable   clear

careful   effective   unbiased   open

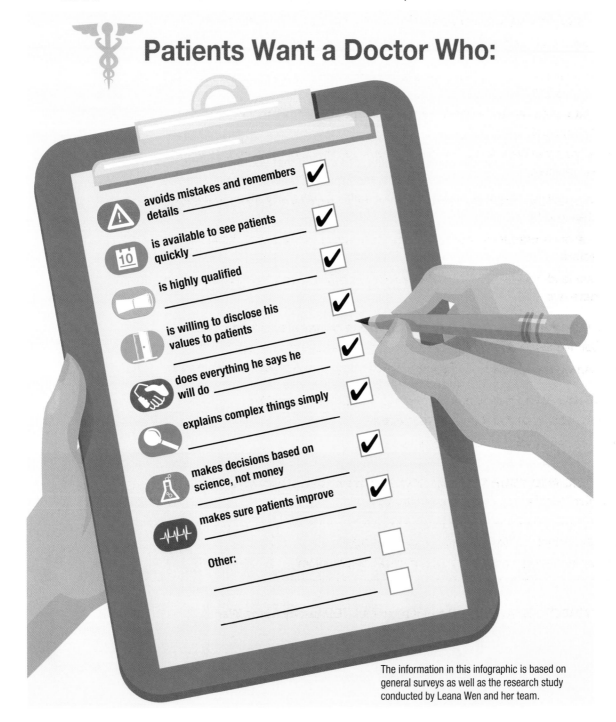

Patients Want a Doctor Who:

avoids mistakes and remembers details ☑

is available to see patients quickly ☑

is highly qualified ☑

is willing to disclose his values to patients ☑

does everything he says he will do ☑

explains complex things simply ☑

makes decisions based on science, not money ☑

makes sure patients improve ☑

Other: ☐

☐

The information in this infographic is based on general surveys as well as the research study conducted by Leana Wen and her team.

L COMMUNICATE Work with a partner. Look at the list in exercise K. Which of the qualities that patients want from their doctors are mentioned by Wen?

M **THINK CRITICALLY** Categorize. Work with a different partner. Look at the infographic on page 37. Match each quality that patients want in a doctor to one of these categories. Write one quality in each blank.

Training: _____ _____

Communication: _____ _____

Behavior: _____ _____

_____ _____

N **THINK CRITICALLY** Reflect. Work with a different partner. Come up with two more qualities that you want in a doctor. Add your ideas to the infographic. Each idea should be an adjective plus a short description. When you have finished, share your ideas with the class.

O **COMMUNICATE** Choose the quality from the infographic that you think is the most important. Then find two partners who each made a different choice. Decide who is student A, student B, and student C. Finally, follow these steps to have short debates with your partners.

Debate 1—Students A and B present their views in turn. Student C decides whose argument was best.

Debate 2—Students B and C present their views in turn. Student A decides whose argument was best.

Debate 3—Students C and A present their views in turn. Student B decides whose argument was best.

Put It Together

A THINK CRITICALLY Synthesize. Work with a partner. Discuss these questions.

1. In the lecture, the professor discusses how social movements can bring about positive social change. What positive social changes do you think Wen's campaign for total transparency in medicine might bring about?

2. In her TED Talk, Wen explains why she thinks patients have the right to know about their doctors. What information would be useful for consumers to know about businesses? What positive changes could result from people knowing this information?

B THINK CRITICALLY Reflect. Work in a small group. Discuss these questions.

1. Has watching Wen's edited TED Talk changed how you think about your doctor? If yes, how have your views changed? If no, why not?

2. What information do you think doctors should be allowed to keep private from their patients? Support your views.

COMMUNICATE

ASSIGNMENT: Have a Team Debate You will have a debate about the topic below. Team A will argue for the topic; Team B will argue against it.

TOPIC The right to privacy is more important than the right to know.

FORMAT Round 1—In turn, a member of Team A and a member of Team B present their team's position.

Round 2—In turn, a second member of each team responds to the other team's position.

Round 3—In turn, a member of each team asks two questions of the other team. The other team responds to the questions.

Round 4—In turn, a member of each team summarizes that team's ideas and views.

Each round lasts up to five minutes. After round 1, teams will have five minutes to discuss how to argue against the ideas that the other team presented. A different member of the team should speak in each round.

PREPARE

PRESENTATION SKILL Give Other People's Points of View

When you give a talk or take part in a debate, giving other people's viewpoints can be effective. You can mention opinions that support your views in order to show the audience that your views have broad support. You can also mention opposing opinions and then say why you disagree with those opinions. You can introduce other people's views in three main ways:

1. Quote somebody's words directly.

   Brandon Combs, an internist in Denver, said, "This has brought me closer to my patients."

2. Summarize somebody's words using reported speech.

   People told me that I'm a traitor to my own profession, that I should be fired.

3. Share research or surveys that give people's views.

   Respondents told us that the doctor-patient relationship is a deeply intimate one.

C COLLABORATE Your teacher will assign you to a team. Work on these tasks with your team members.

- Make sure you fully understand the format of the debate.
- Decide which supporting opinions, reasons, and examples you will discuss.
- Do some research to find other people's viewpoints that you could mention to support your ideas.
- Think of what the opposing team will argue and how you could argue against their position.
- Predict which questions the other team might ask, and discuss how to answer them.

D PRACTICE Work with your team members. Complete these tasks.

- Decide which member of your team will be lead speaker in each round.
- Practice what you will say in the round for which you will be the lead speaker.
- Think about which important information you should stress in order to make your points clearly.
- Listen to feedback from your team members about how you could speak more effectively.

E Read the rubric on page 179. Notice how your debate will be evaluated. Keep these categories in mind as you take part in the debate.

DEBATE

F Have the team debate. Your teacher will act as the timekeeper and moderator. If it is not your turn to speak, listen to what other students are saying. You can quote or use their words when it is your turn to speak. After the debate, provide feedback using the rubric as a guide. Add notes or any other feedback you want to share.

G **THINK CRITICALLY** Evaluate. Work with the members of your team and the opposing team. Discuss what each team did well and what each team could do to make their arguments even stronger. Say what you learned from participating in the debate.

REFLECT

Reflect on what you have learned. Check [✓] your progress.

I can
☐ focus on dates and events when taking notes.
☐ listen for multiple viewpoints about the same topic.
☐ use and understand figurative language.
☐ stress important information.
☐ give other people's points of view when debating or presenting.

I understand the meanings of these words and can use them.
Circle those you know. Underline those you need to work on.

affiliation	expenses	mistrust	respondent AWL
ashamed of	incentive AWL	on behalf of	revelation
collapse AWL	initiative AWL	physician	specialty
controversial AWL	institution AWL	prescribed	transparent
disclose	investigation AWL	pursue AWL	vulnerable

Listen Up!

Coach Aimee Boorman listens to the ideas of
U.S. Olympic gymnast Simone Biles.

THINK AND DISCUSS

1 Read the unit title and look at the photo. A coach might say "Listen up" before speaking to tell her athletes to listen carefully to important information. What other people might say "Listen up," and when and to whom might they say it?

2 In a relationship between a coach and athlete, parent and child, teacher and student, or manager and employee, usually the senior person talks more than he or she listens. What are some advantages and disadvantages of this?

PART 1

The Business of Listening

BEFORE YOU LISTEN

A COMMUNICATE Work with a partner. Discuss these questions.

1. Look at the photo. Journalists use their listening skills daily. What are some other jobs for which listening skills are very important?

2. Studies show that listening is the communication skill people use most but are taught least. Why do you think listening is rarely taught?

3. How would society improve if people received more training in how to listen effectively?

B THINK CRITICALLY Evaluate. Work in a small group. You are going to hear a radio interview with a successful businessperson. Discuss these questions before you listen.

1. How important are each of these skills for businesspeople: speaking, writing, reading, listening? Put the skills in order of importance. Support your point of view.

2. Who do businesspeople need to listen to? Is it important for businesspeople to listen to some people or groups more than others?

Members of the international press listen in on a radio interview at the press center in Geneva, Switzerland.

VOCABULARY

C ⌂ **1.17** Read the definitions of words and phrases from the radio interview. Complete each sentence with one of the bold words or phrases. Then listen to the sentences to check your answers.

a. mentor (n) an experienced person who coaches and advises less experienced people

b. state-of-the-art (adj) having the latest or most up-to-date features

c. recruitment (n) the process of finding and hiring new people to join an organization

d. guidelines (n) general rules or advice for doing something effectively

e. invaluable (adj) extremely useful and/or valuable

f. influential (adj) having a significant influence on something or somebody

g. conscious (adj) choosing to do something intentionally

h. appreciate (v) understand the value of something or somebody, or be thankful

i. rationale (n) the reason(s) for doing something or for making a decision about something

j. ulterior motive (n) a secret reason for doing or saying something

1. After seeing how it led to more sales, the manager could really _____ her team's hard work.

2. At first, the _____ for the firm's choice was unclear, but the reason soon became obvious.

3. Consumers often find the opinions of friends highly _____ when deciding what to purchase.

4. Despite knowing that sales might decline, the company made a _____ decision to raise prices.

5. In order to hire the best new employees, the firm significantly increased its budget for _____ .

6. The company decided to assign junior employees an experienced _____ to give them advice.

7. The company's computers were _____; none of its competitors had such advanced machines.

8. The company developed a set of written _____ to help new employees learn the job quickly.

9. The executive's ability to speak three languages was an _____ skill when traveling on business.

10. The manager suspected that the staff member had an _____ for requesting extra time off.

D COMMUNICATE Discuss these questions with a partner. Use a form of the bold word when you answer each question.

1. Would you feel comfortable acting as a **mentor** to somebody else? Why, or why not?

2. Think of something you can do well. What **guidelines** do you follow when you do it?

3. What is the most **invaluable** piece of advice that anyone has ever given you?

4. Name one person who has been very **influential** in your life. In what ways did this person have an effect on you?

5. Think of a time when you made a **conscious** decision to do something. What did you decide to do, and why?

6. What is one thing you **appreciate** because you understand its value?

LISTEN

E 🎧 **1.18 LISTEN FOR MAIN IDEAS** Listen to the radio interview. Then discuss with a partner which three statements Sandra Davies would completely agree with and check (✓) those answers.

1. _____ Both content-focused and people-focused listening have benefits.

2. _____ Even though listening seems easy, not everybody can do it well.

3. _____ Everyone should have a mentor when they start out in business.

4. _____ Listening carefully to others is a valuable skill that can lead to success.

5. _____ The only way to learn to listen well is to read books about listening.

NOTE-TAKING SKILL Note the Sequence of Events

It is often important to note the sequence in which events or stages in a process happen.

To note the sequence of events, listen for verb tenses and other markers such as *before, first, and then, after that,* or *lastly.* You don't need to make a note of the markers you hear. Instead, use the markers to help you number the points in your notes so the order of events is clear.

Script:

*"I worked for many years **before** I quit my job and started my own business. **First**, I worked in sales, **and then** in a cafe, and, **lastly**, I spent six years at a software company."*

Notes:

④ quit job ➔ started own busns
① sales
② cafe
③ 6 yrs at softwr co

F 🎧 **1.19 LISTEN FOR DETAILS** Listen to segment 2 of the radio interview and take notes. Then use your notes to indicate the order (1–7) in which the events happened in these sample notes.

_____ *Sandra Davies (SD) almost loses job due to poor listening*

_____ *SD asks to get coffee machine (CM), boss gives big bdgt*

_____ *SD orders $$$ CM f/ Italy*

_____ *SD srprsd by size of bdgt but not confirm w/ boss*

_____ *CM arrives and SD makes coffee for boss*

_____ *SD learns boss wanted copier not CM*

_____ *SD not lose job b/c cmpny saves $$$ on rcrtmnt*

G THINK CRITICALLY Interpret. Work with a partner. Answer these questions about the sample notes in exercise F.

1. How do you know what the abbreviations *SD* and *CM* mean?

2. Do you think the abbreviation *$$$* has the same meaning both times it is used?

3. What do the abbreviations *f/*, *w/*, and *b/c* probably mean?

4. How are the words *budget, surprised, company,* and *recruitment* abbreviated?

LISTENING SKILL Draw Conclusions

Speakers sometimes imply ideas without stating them directly. In such cases, you must infer, or draw a conclusion about, their points. Read the following exchange.

Woman: *I wish I were a better listener.*

Man: *I felt like that until I found an online talk with some great ideas. I'll send you the link.*

To draw a conclusion, think about:

1. What the speaker might have left out

The man does not say the online talk has *"ideas about being a better listener."* However, we can come to this conclusion because, otherwise, he would have no reason to mention the talk.

2. Why the speaker is saying something

The man says he will send a link to the online talk after the woman says she wants to be a better listener. We can reach the conclusion that he says this to recommend that she watch the talk.

H 🎧 **1.20** Listen to segment 3, which includes three excerpts from the radio interview. Check (✓) the conclusion(s) you can draw from each excerpt.

1a. _____ Sandra Davies believes that she benefited from the advice given by her mentor.

1b. _____ Davies thinks young people typically do not listen to advice they are given.

2a. _____ Davies was concerned that her boss might limit her responsibility.

2b. _____ Davies was surprised by the size of the budget she had to spend.

3a. _____ Davies thinks some listeners to the broadcast might want to check out Julian Treasure.

3b. _____ Davies feels that leaders who are not good at listening find it hard to influence others.

AFTER YOU LISTEN

I **COMMUNICATE** Work in a small group. Discuss these questions.

1. In the radio interview, Sandra Davies implies that young people typically ignore advice they are given. Do you agree that young people often ignore advice? If so, why? If you disagree, support your view.

2. Davies also says that *"Listening is something that everyone knows how to do because it's a natural skill, but that doesn't mean everyone can do it well."* Do you agree that not everyone can listen well? Why, or why not?

3. Davies also discusses Julian Treasure's idea that *"Great leaders, the people who are the most influential, are usually really good at listening to others."* Do you agree? Why, or why not?

J **THINK CRITICALLY** Reflect. Work in a small group. Study the information about listening styles on page 49. Then discuss these questions.

1. Which two of these listening styles does Sandra Davies discuss? Which one is her usual style?

2. Which listening style sounds like your natural style? Do you always use this style? Why, or why not?

3. What are some advantages and disadvantages of each listening style?

WHAT IS YOUR LISTENING STYLE?

 CONTENT-FOCUSED listeners focus on facts and details. They prefer listening to people with expert knowledge of a subject, and may not accept information unsupported by evidence.

ACTION-FOCUSED listeners focus on why communication is happening and what actions will result from it. They prefer listening to people who speak clearly and accurately.

 PEOPLE-FOCUSED listeners focus on other people's emotions and concerns. They want to build relationships and find connections with others, and use listening as a way to do that.

TIME-FOCUSED listeners focus on how long communication takes. They prefer listening to people who get to the point quickly, and may set a time limit for the person speaking.

Sources: Changing Minds.org; Innolect, Inc.; Management Training Specialists

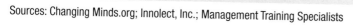

SPEAKING

SPEAKING SKILL Use Humor

Humor can make a speaker more enjoyable, engaging, and memorable for listeners. In general, there are two ways to be funny. Often a speaker will use both ways at the same time:

1. Say something humorous (e.g., say something unexpected and funny, or tell a joke or amusing story).

2. Say something humorously (e.g., use amusing intonation, or comical facial expressions and gestures).

Studies show that most humor comes from saying something that is unexpected or breaks the rules but is not threatening. As a result, it is important to be careful when using humor because saying something that is supposed to be humorous but that listeners do not find funny can cause people to feel uncomfortable. And using too much humor can take the focus away from the main message.

K 🎧 **1.19 COMMUNICATE** Work in a small group. Listen again to segment 2 of the radio interview. Then discuss the questions.

1. In your view, does Sandra Davies use both ways of being funny described in the skills box? Support your opinion.

2. Does her use of humor make her words more enjoyable, engaging, and memorable for you? Why, or why not?

3. Do you think her use of humor could make people uncomfortable or take away from her main message? Why, or why not?

4. Do you generally use humor when you communicate in English? Why, or why not?

L COMMUNICATE Interview several other students. Ask about a funny story that happened to them and tell a funny story that happened to you.

A: *Can you tell me a funny story that happened to you?*

B: *Well, last week a woman asked me if I had a dime. I told her that I didn't have any money, but actually she just wanted to know what time it was! I was very embarrassed!*

PRONUNCIATION SKILL Intonation for Lists

When speakers mention several items, ideas, or events in a short sequence, they often say them as a list. Each item in an open list should have a rising intonation. If the speaker closes the list by saying *and* or *or* before the final item or uses a phrase like *and so on* or *among others,* the final item will have a falling intonation.

1.21

Open list: For me, effective listening involves observing, thinking, asking questions.

Closed list: I like watching funny movies, listening to funny radio shows, and so on.

M 1.22 Draw arrows to mark whether each list item in these excerpts from the radio interview should have rising or falling intonation. Then listen and check your answers.

1. *"My poor listening skills had almost cost me my job, so I read books about listening, watched talks about listening, asked people questions about listening."*

2. *"So the acronym RASA stands for receive, appreciate, summarize, and ask."*

3. *"This means that I want to hear facts, data, or evidence so that I can make an informed judgment about what I'm hearing."*

4. *"This means that I listen for feelings, for things I have in common with the other person, and so on."*

N COMMUNICATE Work with a partner. Tell your partner the names of the people you interviewed in exercise L. Then say which three students told the funniest stories and why. Be sure to use the correct rising or falling intonation when you give lists of names.

I interviewed Marta, Junichi, Khaled, Sofia, So-young. I liked Junichi's story because . . .

Want to help someone? Shut up and listen!

❝ I do something very, very, very difficult. I shut up and listen. **❞**

BEFORE YOU WATCH

A COMMUNICATE Work in a small group. Read the title of the TED Talk and the information about the speaker. Then discuss these questions.

1. From the title of his talk, what conclusions can you draw about Ernesto Sirolli's beliefs about listening?

2. Do you think Sirolli is being serious or joking when he says that it is "very, very, very difficult" to "shut up and listen"? Why?

3. Are there any examples of sustainable community projects in your area? If so, describe them; if not, what projects do you think your community needs?

ERNESTO SIROLLI Sustainable Development Expert

Ernesto Sirolli is an influential expert in sustainable economic development, which means development that improves people's lives but does not use up natural resources. In 1985, he developed a unique method of helping people by building on their passion, determination, intelligence, and skills. Sirolli calls this method "Enterprise Facilitation." He founded the Sirolli Institute, an international non-profit organization that provides business management and networking advice, and gives leaders an effective way to improve their communities.

Ernesto Sirolli's idea worth spreading is that helping others must begin with listening to them.

B COMMUNICATE Work in a small group. Take turns responding to these questions.

1. Describe a situation when somebody helped you succeed by listening to you.

2. Have you ever found it hard to "shut up and listen" to another person? Explain.

VOCABULARY

C 🎧 1.23 These definitions will help you learn words in the TED Talk. Add one of the bold words to each blank to complete the sentences below. Then listen to the sentences to check your answers.

a. **enterprise** (n) a project or company, especially a new one that requires hard work

b. **facilitator** (n) a person who helps somebody by making an action or process easier

c. **capturing** (v) taking something in order to use it or to hold the attention of somebody

d. **initiate** (v) cause an action or process to start or a project to be launched

e. **dedicated** (adj) describing people who put a great deal of time or energy into something

f. **servant** (n) a person who performs duties for others, such as household tasks

g. **infrastructure** (n) basic things like equipment and power needed for society or a project

h. **activate** (v) make something active or start working, or start something moving forward

i. **make a living** (v) earn enough money from work to pay for all the things one needs

j. **confidentiality** (n) the state of keeping information or ideas secret or private

1. Despite having no formal training as a _____,
Emma was great at making things easy for clients. And she was so
_____ to helping them succeed that she made herself
available to answer questions on weekends and in the evenings.

2. Soon after Marek started an _____, the economy collapsed
and he was worried about being able to _____. With a lot of
hard work, however, he turned it into a very successful and profitable company.

3. To compete effectively with other firms, the company invested heavily
in upgrading its _____. It also focused on
_____ good ideas from staff and using them to improve its
efficiency.

4. In his role as a domestic _____, Jack learned some
private information about his employers. He took pride in maintaining
_____, however, and never disclosed any of their secrets.

5. The government decided to _____ a policy to help citizens
launch small businesses. It took six months of hard work before government
officials were able to _____ the new policy and start helping
the first entrepreneurs.

Tokyo's infrastructure includes train tracks, bridges, and tunnels.

D COMMUNICATE Work in a small group. Discuss the questions. Use the bold words when you discuss.

1. In what ways do computers **facilitate** our lives, and in what ways, if any, do they make them harder?

2. What was the last thing that **captured** your attention? Why?

3. If you had the money and resources to **initiate** any project you liked, what would you do? Why?

4. Describe someone you know who is **dedicated** to a person, a cause, or their profession. How do they show their dedication?

5. It has been said that to be a good leader, one must first be a good **servant.** Do you agree with this idea? Why, or why not?

6. The photo and caption show and describe the **infrastructure** of Tokyo. What does the infrastructure of a company consist of?

7. What are some interesting ways for people to **make a living** that you have heard of? Would you like to do these jobs? Why, or why not?

8. For which jobs is **confidentiality** a requirement? Why is it so important for these jobs?

WATCH

E ▶ **1.11** **WATCH FOR MAIN IDEAS** Watch segments 1, 2, 3, and 4 from the edited TED Talk. Choose the letter of the phrase that describes Sirolli's main purpose in each segment. Two phrases won't be used.

1. Segment 1 _____

2. Segment 2 _____

3. Segment 3 _____

4. Segment 4 _____

a. to describe a situation that changed his way of thinking

b. to explain how his method can improve local communities

c. to give specific examples of clients whom his method has helped

d. to name the people who influenced him early in his career

e. to introduce a method for helping people that he developed

f. to summarize why so few people are successful entrepreneurs

F ▶**1.12** **WATCH FOR DETAILS** Watch segment 3 again. Complete each statement by writing in the two missing details.

> $15 per kilo   27 projects   300 communities
> 40,000 businesses   first client   five fishermen
> one year   three days

1. Ernesto Sirolli found his _____ after _____ in Esperance in Western Australia.

2. Sirolli helped _____ sell tuna to Japan for _____ instead of 60 cents per kilo.

3. In _____, Sirolli was working on _____, and the government asked for his advice.

4. Sirolli and his team have started _____ in _____ around the globe.

G ▶**1.13** **DRAW CONCLUSIONS** Watch segment 5, which includes three excerpts from the edited TED Talk. Does each answer summarize something Sirolli states directly, or is it a conclusion you can draw? Write D for *directly stated* points or C for *conclusions*.

1a. _____ Ernesto Sirolli has written more than one book.

1b. _____ The Italians thought money would motivate people.

2a. _____ Sirolli helped some people sell their products overseas at a much higher price.

2b. _____ The people Sirolli helped were spreading the word about what he could do.

3a. _____ Entrepreneurs are concerned about sharing information about their business ideas.

3b. _____ Entrepreneurs will not work with people unless they promise to keep their secrets.

H ▶**1.13** **THINK CRITICALLY** **Analyze.** Work in a small group. Compare your answers to exercise G. Then watch segment 5 again. Discuss the clues that helped you draw conclusions from the points that Sirolli made indirectly.

WORDS IN THE TALK
cannery (n): a factory where food is put into cans
distraught (adj): extremely upset
Maori (adj): a member of the native population of New Zealand
tremendous (adj): excellent, fantastic, very good

I ▶ **1.14** **WATCH FOR HUMOR** Work with a partner. Watch segment 6, which includes excerpts from the edited TED Talk. Discuss why each excerpt is funny and check (✓) the reason(s).

	Sirolli Says Something Humorous	Sirolli Says Something Humorously
1. Excerpt 1	☐	☐
2. Excerpt 2	☐	☐
3. Excerpt 3	☐	☐
4. Excerpt 4	☐	☐
5. Excerpt 5	☐	☐

J **THINK CRITICALLY** Evaluate. Work with a partner. Discuss these questions.

1. How amusing did you find Ernesto Sirolli's TED Talk? Why?

2. Which excerpt in exercise I did you find the funniest? Why?

3. To what extent did his use of humor influence your feelings about him and his talk?

4. Did his use of humor make his overall message stronger? Why, or why not?

K ▶ **1.15** **EXPAND YOUR VOCABULARY** Watch the excerpts from the TED Talk. Guess the meanings the phrases in the box.

> shaped by   in the nick of time   blunder around
>
> one-on-one   tryout

L **WATCH MORE** Go to TED.com to watch the full TED talk by Ernesto Sirolli.

17 Global Goals for Sustainable Development

 1 No poverty

 2 _____

 3 Good health & well being

 4 Quality education

 5 _____

 6 _____

 7 Affordable & clean energy

 8 Decent work & economic growth

 9 Industry, innovation, & infrastructure

 10 Reduced inequalities

 11 Sustainable cities & communities

 12 Responsible consumption & production

 13 _____

 14 _____

 15 Life on land

 16 Peace & strong social institutions

17 _____

Source: United Nations

M THINK CRITICALLY Interpret an Infographic. Work with a partner. Add the missing labels to the infographic from the choices below. When you have finished, compare answers with another pair of students.

a. Climate action

b. Gender equality

c. Clean water and sanitation

d. Partnerships for the goals

e. Life below water

f. Zero hunger

N **THINK CRITICALLY** **Evaluate.** Work in a small group. Sirolli's idea of Enterprise Facilitation is clearly related to goal 8 in the infographic on page 57. Which of the other goals is his work related to?

O **THINK CRITICALLY** **Identify.** Work in a small group. One of the Global Goals for Sustainable Development from the infographic is "Quality education". What sub-goals are necessary to meet this goal? Discuss your ideas and add them to the chart below. Then share your thoughts with another group.

A: *For me, quality education depends on quality teachers.*

B: *Right! So I guess teacher training would be an important sub-goal.*

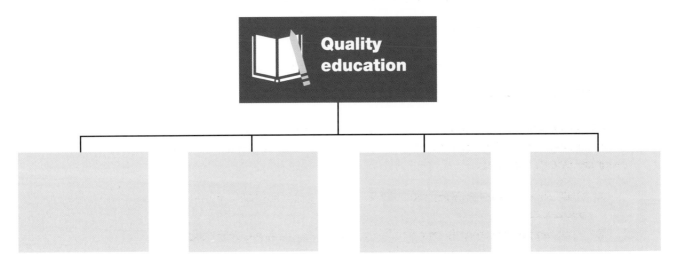

P **COLLABORATE** Work with a partner. Follow these steps.

1. Choose one of the other Global Goals for Sustainable Development from the infographic.

2. Imagine that your job is to initiate action to meet this goal. Identify at least three organizations or groups of people to whom you should listen in order to get information to meet that goal successfully.

3. Join another pair of students. Tell them the names of the organizations or people you identified in step 2, but do not tell them which goal you chose in step 1. Ask them if they can guess which goal you chose based on the names.

Put It Together

A THINK CRITICALLY Synthesize. Work with a partner. Read the six opinions below. Then write *Interview* if you heard this opinion during the radio interview in Part 1, *TED Talk* if Ernesto Sirolli expressed the opinion in his talk, or *Both* if you heard the opinion in both.

1. Effective listening involves not speaking. _____

2. Good listening leads to good relationships. _____

3. It can be difficult to listen to other people. _____

4. Listening is an effective way to help others. _____

5. Not listening to others can cause mistakes. _____

6. There are various ways to listen effectively. _____

B COMMUNICATE Work in a small group. Discuss ways in which good listening skills can help you deliver effective presentations. When you have finished, share your ideas with the class.

A: *Well, it's obviously important to listen carefully to questions from the audience.*

B: *Yeah, and listening to feedback after rehearsing a talk is essential, too.*

COMMUNICATE

ASSIGNMENT: Give a Pair Presentation Work with a partner to deliver a presentation about the benefits of listening. Choose from one of these pairs of people or groups, or come up with one of your own. You can also reverse the order and discuss, for example, how parents might benefit if children listened to them. Discuss how:

Children		parents	
Students		teachers	
Customers	might benefit if	companies	shut up and listened to them.
Patients		doctors	
Your idea		your idea	

PREPARE

PRESENTATION SKILL Use Gestures

Using gestures is a natural and effective way to emphasize and clarify specific aspects of your spoken message in a nonverbal way. Generally speaking, there are four types of gestures. These are often used in combination with facial expressions:

1. *Descriptive:* spreading your hands apart to show length or time; moving your hand up or down to suggest an increase or decrease

2. *Emotional:* holding your hand to your heart to show passion; raising your arms and jumping in the air to show happiness

3. *Symbolic:* holding up your hand to signify the idea of stopping; using your fingers to show how many points you are going to make

4. *Illustrative:* pretending to eat something or typing in the air with your hands to illustrate the act of eating or typing

C ▶ **1.16** Watch segment 4 of the edited TED Talk again. Ask your teacher to pause the video when you see Sirolli make an interesting gesture. Discuss the type, purpose, and value of each gesture.

D **COLLABORATE** Work with your partner. Discuss ideas for your presentation. Focus on the following:

- Which two or three benefits you should mention in your talk
- Gestures that might emphasize and clarify your ideas
- Humor you could use to make your talk interesting
- Which parts of your talk each of you will present

E **COLLABORATE** Work with your partner. Practice delivering your presentation until you feel you can deliver it confidently and fluently.

F Read the rubric on page 180. Notice how your presentation will be evaluated. Keep these categories in mind as you present.

PRESENT

G Give your presentation to the class. Watch your classmates' presentations and listen carefully. Ask any questions you may have after each presentation.

H **THINK CRITICALLY** Evaluate. Work with a different partner. Listen carefully to your partner's feedback about the strengths of your presentation. Ask questions and give your own feelings about your talk. Then switch roles.

REFLECT

Reflect on what you have learned. Check [✓] your progress.

I can
- ☐ note the sequence of events or ideas that a speaker mentions.
- ☐ draw conclusions about points that a speaker mentions indirectly.
- ☐ recognize and use humor when talking or giving a speech.
- ☐ use the correct rising or falling intonation when listing items.
- ☐ use gestures to provide nonverbal support for my words.

I understand the meanings of these words and can use them.
Circle those you know. Underline those you need to work on.

activate	dedicated	infrastructure AWL	rationale
appreciate AWL	enterprise	initiate AWL	recruitment
capture	facilitation AWL	invaluable	servant
confidentiality	guidelines AWL	make a living	state-of-the-art
conscious	influential	mentor	ulterior motive

lt_profile_image":false,"following":null,"follow_request_
ions":null),"geo":null,"coordinates":null,"place":
7d","url":"https://api.twitter.com/1.1/geo/id/88be0e4ebe3
pe":"city","name":"Poplar","full_name":"Poplar,
"GB","country":"United Kingdom","bounding_box":
ordinates":[[[-0.000028,51.48432],[-0.000028,51.545341],
[0.000989,51.48432]]]),"attributes":
ll,"is_quote_status":false,"retweet_count":0,"favorite_co
shtags":[],"urls":
/m01DyG0ikb","expanded_url":"http://bit.ly/1VEQjo4","disp
jo4","indices":[64,87])],"user_mentions":[],"symbols":
"retweeted":false,"possibly_sitive":false,"filter_lev
"timestamp_ms":"14490448731   "sentiment_score":0)

#bestshot #foodlover
#uk"),"comments":{"count":0,"data":
[]),"created_time":"1449044866","filter":"Normal","id":"113099277
993158","images":{"low_resolution":
{"height":320,"url":"https://scontent.cdninstagram.com/hphotos-xt
15/s320x320/e35/12331877_137980019900821_867434971_n.jpg","width"
rd_resolution":{"height":640,"url":"https://scontent.cdninstagram
xtp1/t51.2885-
15/s640x640/sh0.08/e35/12331877_137980019900821_867434971_n.jpg","
"thumbnail":{"height":150,"url":"https://scontent.cdninstagram.co
xtp1/t51.2885-
15/s150x150/e35/12331877_137980019900821_867434971_n.jpg","width"
":{"count":0,"data":[]),"link":"https://www.instagram.com/p/-yF-
9oMV8F/","location":
{"id":220127119,"latitude":51.510166565,"longitude":-0.197455731
ng Hill, Portobello Road Market"),"tags":
["bestshot","trendsetter","igworldclub","jetsetter","awesome","p
isgood","journey","london","adventure","instatravel","trip","ins
erlust","lifestyle","travelblogger"   theworld",
l_shots","foodlover","travelblog,   "uk","travelgram"
oliday","fashionista","travel"],"   "user":
{"full_name":"P.R.D.A.S.V.M.N","i   "profile_picture":
ent.cdninstagram.com/hphotos-xat1/
19/s150x150/12081090_1696823697203   021_a.jpg","usernam
da"),"user_has_liked":false,"users_   :[]}

02T08:27:15.212Z", "timeToStation":0, "timestamp":"2015-12-
02T08:27:15.212Z", "towards":"Brixton", "vehicleId":"242"},
{"$type":"Tfl.Api.Presentation.Entities.Prediction,
Tfl.Api.Presentation.Entities", "currentLocation":"At
Platform", "destinationName":"Brixton Underground
Station", "destinationNaptanId":"940GZZLUBXN", "direction":"inbound
rival":"2015-12-
02T08:27:15.369Z", "id":"1114957168", "lineId":"victoria", "lineName
modeName":"tube", "naptanId":"940GZZLUWRR", "operationType":1, "pla
outhbound - Platform 4", "stationName":"Warren Street Underground
Station", "timeToLive":"2015-12-
02T08:27:15.369Z", "timeToStation":0, "timestamp":"2015-12-
02T08:27:15.369Z", "towards":"Brixton", "vehicleId":"236"},
{"$type":"Tfl.Api.Presentation.Entities.Prediction,
Tfl.Api.Presentation.Entities", "currentLocation":"Between Warren
Oxford Circus", "destinationName":"Walthamstow Central Underground
Station", "destinationNaptanId":"940GZZLUWWL", "direction":"outboun
rrival":"2015-12-
02T08:27:42.306Z", "id":"-326348385", "lineId":"victoria", "lineNam
modeName":"tube", "naptanId":"940GZZLUWRR", "operationType":1, "pl
orthbound - Platform 3", "stationName":"Warren Street Underground
Station", "timeToLive":"2015-12-
02T08:27:42.306Z", "timeToStation":27, "timestamp":"2015-12-
02T08:27:15.306Z", "towards":"Walthamstow Central", "vehicleId":"2
{"$type":"Tfl.Api.Presentation.Entities.Prediction,
Tfl.Api.Presentation.Entities", "currentLocation":"At
Platform", "destinationName":"Bank Underground
Station", "destinationNaptanId":"940GZZLUBNK", "expectedArrival":"
02T08:27:43.509Z", "id":"1723383418", "lineId":"waterloo-
ity", "lineName":"Waterloo &
City", "modeName":"tube", "naptanId":"940GZZLUBNK", "operationType
e":"Westbound - Platform 7", "stationName":"Bank Underground
Station", "timeToLive":"2015-12-
02T08:27:43.509Z", "timeToStation":0, "timestamp":"2015-12-
02T08:27:43.509Z", "towards":"Bank", "vehicleId":"203"},
{"$type":"Tfl.Api.Presentation.Entities.Prediction,
Tfl.Api.Presentation.Entities", "currentLocation":"At
Platform", "destinationName":"Waterloo Underground
Station", "destinationNaptanId":"940GZZLUWLO", "expectedArrival":
02T08:27:43.634Z", "id":"1789781517", "lineId":"waterloo-
ity", "lineName":"Waterloo &
City", "modeName":"tube", "naptanId":"940GZZLUWLO", "operationType
e":"Westbound Platform 26", "stationName":"Waterloo Underground
Station", "timeToLive":"2015-12-
02T08:27:43.634Z", "timeToStation":0, "timestamp":"2015-12-
02T08:27:43.634Z", "towards":"Waterloo", "vehicleId":"205"},
{"$type":"Tfl.Api.Presentation.Entities.Prediction,
Tfl.Api.Presentation.Entities", "currentLocation":"At
Platform", "destinationName":"Bank Underground
Station", "destinationNaptanId":"940GZZLUBNK", "direction":"outb
rrival":"2015-12-02T08:27:43.634Z", "id":"1924610172", "lineId":
ity", "lineName":"Waterloo &
City", "modeName":"tube", "naptanId":"940GZZLUWLO", "operationTyp
e":"Eastbound Platform 25", "stationName":"Waterloo Undergroun
Station", "timeToLive":"2015-12-
02T08:27:43.634Z", "timeToStation":0, "timestamp":"2015-12-
02T08:27:43.634Z", "towards":"Bank", "vehicleId":"202"}]}

A man walks in front of a data feed at Big Bang Data,
an exhibition in London, England, that explores how the
huge increase of available data is changing our lives.

THINK AND DISCUSS

1 Look at the photo and read the caption. Does the photo give you a positive impression about the "huge increase" of data that "is changing our lives"? Why, or why not?

2 Big data can be defined as very large amounts of information that companies use to produce new goods and services. What kinds of information do companies know about you? How did they learn it? How do you feel about them knowing it?

Datatainment

BEFORE YOU LISTEN

A COMMUNICATE Work in a small group. Discuss these questions.

1. The term "datatainment" is made up from two other words. What are those two words, and what do you think the term means?

2. Look at the photo. Do you think it illustrates the idea of datatainment? If yes, how does it illustrate it? If no, what kind of photo would illustrate the idea better?

B COMMUNICATE Work with a partner. You are going to hear a sociology professor lecture about the impact of big data on the entertainment industry. Predict which forms of entertainment she might discuss. Are these forms of entertainment popular in your country? Why, or why not?

Time for ball to reach goal
8/10 of a second

German goalkeeper Timo
Horn reaction time
1/10 of a second

BRA　0
GER　0
26:19　1ST

Speed of ball
70 mph

Spin rate of ball
500 rpm

Distance from goal
30 yards

Brazilian attacker Neymar
2016 Olympics
**goals scored: 4
minutes played: 570**

VOCABULARY

C 🎧 **1.24** Read these definitions of words from the lecture. Then choose the correct word in parentheses to complete each sentence below. Finally, listen and check your answers.

a. **commerce** (n) the buying or selling of goods or services, especially on a large scale

b. **customize** (v) modify something to make it better for a specific person or situation

c. **demographic** (n) a specific group within a population, such as women in their 20s

d. **formula** (n) a conventional method of doing something that often follows a pattern

e. **log** (v) make a systematic record of various measurements or data

f. **notable** (adj) especially important, impressive, or worth noticing

g. **overlook** (v) fail to notice; ignore something

h. **prosper** (v) be successful, especially in financial terms

i. **revolutionary** (adj) related to a complete or dramatic change in something

j. **sector** (n) a division of society, the population, industry, or a national economy

1. According to data released by the government, the volume of online (*commerce*/*sector*) has increased significantly over the last few years.

2. The film studio thought the movie would be popular among a particular (*demographic*/*formula*) and were surprised to discover that it had a broad appeal.

3. The store used data from customer surveys and online reviews to develop a range of new products that could be (*customized*/*logged*) by shoppers.

4. Film and television are probably the two (*demographics*/*sectors*) of the entertainment industry that generate the most revenue, but video games are very profitable, too.

5. The plot, or story, of many successful movies follows a classic three-part (*commerce*/*formula*): the set up, the confrontation, and the resolution.

6. Using technology, it is relatively easy to (*log*/*overlook*) numerous bits of data about what happens during professional sporting events.

7. As a result of (*customizing*/*overlooking*) how bored consumers were with formulaic dramas, the analysts incorrectly predicted that the new TV show would be popular.

8. The online shopping site (*logged*/*prospered*) after it started using advanced data analytics to give personalized recommendations to its customers.

9. The success of the video game was especially (*notable*/*revolutionary*) because so many people had predicted that it would be a failure.

10. When music producers first began analyzing data about why some songs were successful and others were not, it was (*notable*/*revolutionary*) and transformed the music industry.

D COMMUNICATE Work with a partner. Take turns responding to these questions. Use the bold words in your responses.

1. Do you think that in the future, most **commerce** will take place online? Why, or why not?

2. What kinds of music generally appeal to people in these two **demographics:** teens and college-aged students?

3. Which of these entertainment **sectors** do you enjoy most: movies, books, or video games? Why?

4. What skills do you think people need to **prosper** both academically and professionally?

5. Who are some **notable** people from your country? What is so impressive about them?

6. In your view, what has been the most **revolutionary** change in society in the last decade?

LISTEN

E 🎧 **1.25** ▶ **1.17** **LISTEN FOR MAIN IDEAS** Read these statements, which summarize the key points from the sociology lecture. Then listen to the lecture and number the ideas in the order the professor mentions them.

_____ Although big data has some benefits for film studios, it has disadvantages, too.

_____ Big data has a similar impact on movies as it does on other forms of entertainment.

_____ By analyzing big data, sports teams can find new ways to win and make money.

_____ Studios analyze thousands of people's opinions to predict which films will do well.

_____ The phrase "big data" refers to the way organizations analyze data to produce value.

The Oakland Athletics celebrated a win in their record-breaking 2002 season.

F 🎧 **1.26** **LISTEN FOR DETAILS** Listen to segment 1 and write T for *true* or F for *false* next to each statement. Then work with a partner to correct the false statements.

1. _____ *Moneyball* is a movie about the Oakland Athletics baseball team.

2. _____ During the 2002 season, Oakland had the lowest payroll of any team.

3. _____ Oakland's payroll was 40 percent below the team with the highest payroll.

4. _____ Oakland analyzed baseball data to find players with undervalued skills.

5. _____ During the season, Oakland won many games, including 12 in a row.

6. _____ Oakland's success was so notable that other teams copied their ideas.

LISTENING SKILL Distinguish Facts from Opinions

Recognizing whether a speaker is stating a fact or giving an opinion is important to accurately interpret information you hear. Sometimes speakers use specific phrases to indicate whether they are stating a fact or giving an opinion.

Fact: *is proved by, studies suggest that, the analysis shows that*

Opinion: *personally, I find, in my view, to my mind*

Often the speaker will not use specific phrases, but you can infer whether he is stating a fact or opinion. A fact is something objective that can be proven. In contrast, an opinion is subjective; it's a personal belief that cannot be proven and that some people might disagree with. If the speaker uses qualitative adjectives such as *main* or *the most important*, most likely it is an opinion.

Fact: *The team won 20 games in a row.*

Opinion: *This is absolutely the best team ever.*

G **COMMUNICATE** Work with a partner. Look at this excerpt from the lecture. Discuss which facts and opinions the professor expresses. Draw a line under facts and a double line under opinions.

"Analysis shows that the cost of making and marketing a major studio movie today averages over $100 million. Given the cost, I'm sure you'll agree that hoping for revenue is hardly a good business strategy. Analyzing big data allows studios to predict more accurately whether their next movie is going to be a hit. And I'd say that this is the main reason why big data has become so important."

H 🎧 **1.27** Listen to segment 2, which includes five excerpts from the lecture. Check [✓] whether each excerpt includes a fact, an opinion, or both.

1. fact _____ opinion _____   **4.** fact _____ opinion _____

2. fact _____ opinion _____   **5.** fact _____ opinion _____

3. fact _____ opinion _____

AFTER YOU LISTEN

I **THINK CRITICALLY Evaluate.** Work in a small group. In the lecture, the professor says that many movies are predictable because they follow a formula. To what extent do you think each of these forms of entertainment is predictable? Put them in order from least likely (1) to most likely (5) to follow a formula. Think of examples to support your views. Then share your opinions with the rest of the class.

_____ Books   _____ Movies   _____ Music   _____ TV shows   _____ Video games

J **COMMUNICATE** Work with a partner. Using big data to predict which movies, TV shows, music, and video games are likely to be successful is good for creators of entertainment. In what ways is it also good for consumers? Is it bad for consumers in any way?

SPEAKING

SPEAKING SKILL **Talk about Causal Relationships**

Speakers often need to discuss the causes of an action, event, or situation, or the effects of that same action, event, or situation. There are three common ways to introduce causal relationships. The first two ways make the causal relationship explicit; the third way implies it:

1. Use specific words or phrases to introduce the cause or effect of something.

   Cause: *This is the main reason, This was caused by, because*

   Effect: *As a result, One effect of this was, so*

2. Ask and answer questions.

   Cause: *The reason? Why did this happen? How did this come about?*

   Effect: *What happened? What was the result? The outcome?*

3. Discuss things together, sometimes using time or sequence expressions to show their order.

   They analyzed the data. Profits rose. (implies that profits rose because of the data analysis)

(See page 164 in the *Independent Student Handbook* for more information on talking about causes and effects.)

K THINK CRITICALLY Analyze. Work in a small group. Read the excerpts from the lecture. Then discuss the questions below.

a. *"Analyzing big data allows studios to predict more accurately whether their next movie is going to be a hit. And I'd say that this is the main reason big data has become so important."*

b. *"The A's management team knew they could not afford to pay for the best players, so they decided to analyze that data looking for information that would allow them to be successful at a reasonable cost."*

c. *"So Oakland signed a number of players who had the skills that big data had suggested would lead to team success. And what happened? Well, I'd say the results were pretty amazing."*

d. *"Oakland's success was very notable. Other baseball teams soon began to copy its revolutionary approach to using big data. And these days, big data is having a big impact in most other sports. The reason? Big data allows teams and individual athletes to prosper."*

1. Does each excerpt give the cause of something or the effect of something? Underline the word or phrase that indicates this.
2. What causal relationship(s) are made explicit in each excerpt?
3. In which excerpt does the speaker also imply a causal relationship? What is it?

L COMMUNICATE Work with a partner. Complete these tasks.

1. Think of a causal relationship you are comfortable discussing. For example, you could talk about why you chose to study English at your current school.
2. Share the causal relationship with your partner. Use one or more ways of introducing causal relationships from the skill box.
3. Listen to your partner. Which way(s) of introducing causal relationships does he or she use?

Video games are a popular, and profitable, sector of the entertainment industry.

Compound nouns are nouns that combine two words. A compound noun can be written as one word (*airplane*) or two (*seat belt*). The primary stress is usually on the stressed syllable in the first part of the compound (for one-word compounds) or the stressed syllable in the first word of the compound (for two-word compounds). Listen to these examples:

1.28

> **foot**ball, **smart**phone, uni**ver**sity student, **ad**vertising industry

There are exceptions to this guideline. For example, in two-word compounds that are names, the primary stress may be on the stressed syllable in the second word of the compound. Listen to these examples:

> New **York**, Olympic **Games**, art **his**tory, Industrial Revo**lu**tion

Check a dictionary if you are unsure which syllable to stress.

M **1.29** **COMMUNICATE** Work with a partner. Underline the compound nouns in these excerpts from the lecture. Discuss how you think each compound noun should be pronounced. Then listen to the excerpts to check your answers and mark the stressed part of each compound. Are there any examples of exceptions to the rules in the skills box?

1. *"Today, though, we'll focus on how big data helps the entertainment industry make more money."*

2. *"Film studios can use a wide variety of data about people's opinions. Take social media, for example."*

3. *"Want to know which type of movie is most likely to appeal to 20-year-old college students studying art history in Los Angeles, for example?"*

4. *"No other baseball team won more games than Oakland that year."*

N **COMMUNICATE** Work with a different partner. Take turns responding to these questions. Focus on pronouncing each compound noun correctly.

1. Which of these cities would you most like to visit: Abu Dhabi, Buenos Aires, Hong Kong, or Los Angeles? Why?

2. Which of these foods do you eat most often: apple pie, French fries, ice cream, or seafood? Why?

3. Which of these sports do you most enjoy watching: baseball, basketball, football, or mountain biking? Why?

4. Which of these subjects would you most like to study: art history, business studies, computer science, or gender studies? Why?

Big data is better data

" Big data is an extremely important tool by which society is going to advance. **"**

BEFORE YOU WATCH

A COMMUNICATE Work in a small group. Read the title and information about the TED speaker. Discuss some reasons why "big data is better data." Also discuss why big data might help society advance. Are there any ways in which big data might *not* be better?

KENNETH CUKIER   Journalist and Editor

Kenneth Cukier works as the Data Editor for *The Economist,* a weekly newspaper that covers politics, business, finance, science, and technology, and how they are connected. He has spent years thinking about how big data will affect the future. He is the co-author of *Big Data: A Revolution That Will Transform How We Live, Work, and Think.* According to the *New York Times*, this book is "a fascinating—and sometimes alarming—survey of big data's growing effect on just about everything."

▶ 1.18 THINK CRITICALLY Predict. Work in a small group. Cukier begins his talk by discussing "America's favorite pie." Discuss what type of pie you think this is and why he might have chosen to start his talk in this way. Then watch segment 1 of the edited TED Talk to confirm your ideas.

VOCABULARY

C **⌂ 1.30** These definitions will help you learn words in the TED Talk. Read the definitions. Then choose the correct word in parentheses to complete each sentence below. Finally, listen and check your answers.

a. hype (n) exaggerated statements about the quality or importance of something

b. store (v) keep or save something for use in the future

c. transmit (v) pass something, especially information or data, from place to place

d. process (v) perform a series of steps in order to understand information or data

e. static (adj) stationary; not moving or changing

f. dynamic (adj) constantly changing, moving, or full of energy

g. branch (n) a division of an academic subject

h. trait (n) a quality or characteristic that makes it easy to distinguish somebody or something

i. labor (n) work, especially work that requires tiring physical activity

j. eliminate (v) remove or get rid of something or somebody completely

1. After (*processing* / *transmitting*) the sales data, the employees recognized some key trends.

2. An analysis of sales data helped the company recognize the main (*labor* / *traits*) of its customers.

3. Despite the (*branch* / *hype*) about the movie before it opened, the film was surprisingly bad.

4. Improvements in manufacturing allowed the items to be made faster and with less (*hype* / *labor*).

5. Interpretation of the data suggests sales will remain (*dynamic* / *static*) until October and then rise.

6. No data was lost when the computer crashed, as it had been (*eliminated* / *stored*) on a hard drive.

7. The company (*eliminated* / *processed*) dozens of jobs in overseas offices because of falling sales.

8. The decision to hire only (*dynamic* / *static*), motivated employees was rewarded when profits rose.

9. The student wrote a paper about robotics, which is a (*branch* / *trait*) of computer science.

10. With the new system, data can be (*stored* / *transmitted*) between computers quicker than before.

D **COMMUNICATE** Work with a partner. Take turns answering these questions. Use the bold words in your responses.

1. What kinds of things receive **hype** before they are released? In your view, do they generally live up to the hype? Support your opinion.

2. Where do you **store** your passwords?

3. How do you **process** new vocabulary? In other words, what steps do you take to learn new words?

4. What is something in your life that has remained **static** recently? Why has it not changed?

5. What are different **branches** within the academic subject area you are interested in?

6. Think about the job you want in the future. What **traits** might help you be successful in this job?

7. What is something you have done that took a lot of **labor** but was definitely worth the effort?

8. What is something you would like to **eliminate** from your life? Why do you want to get rid of it?

WATCH

learn**more** The Industrial Revolution began around 1760 in Great Britain. New manufacturing processes were developed, and more people began to work in factories. Because these jobs required manual labor, workers would get dirty. They often wore dark clothes to hide the dirt. Jobs like these became known as blue-collar jobs. Today, many people have so-called white-collar jobs that require them to use knowledge rather than perform physical labor.

E ▶ **1.19** **WATCH FOR MAIN IDEAS** Read these statements. Then watch the edited TED Talk. Write MI if a statement is a *main idea* from the talk, or SD if it is a *supporting detail.*

1. _MI_ Big data has the potential to solve serious problems facing society.

2. _SD_ Searching, copying, and sharing information is easier now.

3. _MI_ Machine learning is a valuable tool that has already benefited society.

4. _MI_ Some effects of big data will be negative ones that we must adjust to.

5. _SD_ During the Industrial Revolution, society experienced many changes.

6. _MI_ Having more data allows us to make better, more informed decisions.

F ▶ **1.20** **WATCH FOR DETAILS** Read the information about machine learning. Then watch segment 2 of the edited TED Talk. Check (✓) the information that Cukier mentions. One answer has been done for you.

_✓_ Machine learning is a field of computer science that is related to artificial intelligence.

_____ There are two main kinds of machine learning: supervised and unsupervised learning.

_✓_ The field began in the 50s when Arthur Samuel programmed a computer to learn to play checkers.

_✓_ The basic principle of machine learning is to give data to computers and let them infer rules from it.

_✓_ Machine learning has many beneficial applications, including helping doctors identify cancer cells.

_✓_ Many things we do with technology, such as searching the Internet, rely on machine learning.

WORDS IN THE TALK

algorithm (n): a set of rules a computer follows to calculate something or solve a problem
biopsy (n): a medical examination of material removed from a body to look for a disease
inscriptions (n): words or signs that are cut into rock or metal to create a permanent message
primitive (adj): belonging to an early stage of development

G ▶ **1.21** **DISTINGUISH FACTS FROM OPINIONS** Watch segment 3, which includes six excerpts from the TED Talk. Check [✓] whether each excerpt gives a fact, an opinion, or both.

1. fact ____✓____ opinion _____

2. fact _____ opinion ____✓____

3. fact ____✓____ opinion _____

4. fact ____✓____ opinion ____✓____

5. fact _____ opinion ____✓____

6. fact _____ opinion ____✓____

H ▶ **1.21** **THINK CRITICALLY** Analyze. Work in a small group. Compare your answers to exercise G. Then watch segment 3 again. What clues in each excerpt helped you distinguish facts from opinions?

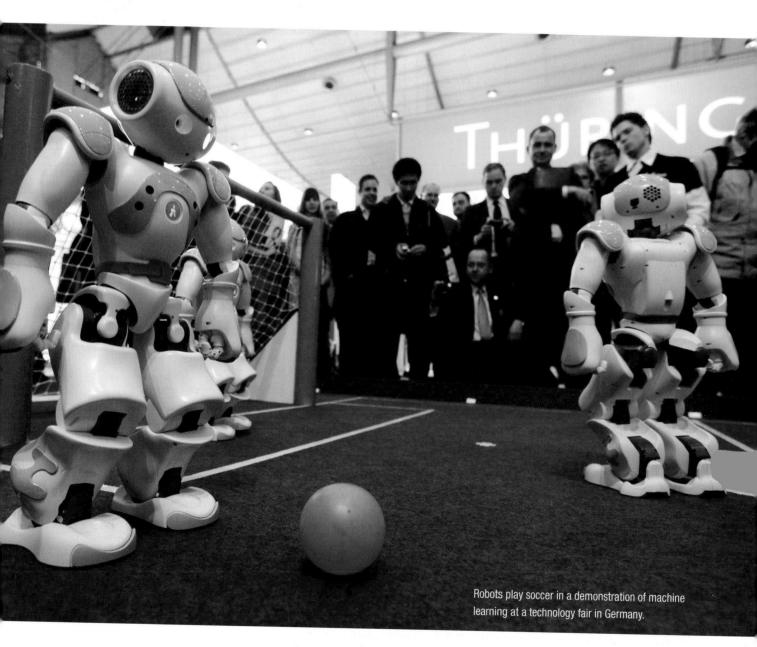

Robots play soccer in a demonstration of machine learning at a technology fair in Germany.

NOTE-TAKING SKILL	Note Causes and Effects

Recognizing causes and effects will help you understand a speaker's ideas. When you take notes, make a note of any causal relationships you hear by drawing an arrow from the cause (or reason) toward the effect (or result).

Examples: *give computer a lot of data* → *computer learns rules from data*

white-collar jobs now common ← *advances in technology*

(See page 169 in the *Independent Student Handbook* for more information about organizing your notes to show causes and effects.)

I **▶ 1.22 WATCH AND NOTE CAUSES AND EFFECTS** Watch segment 4, which includes excerpts from the edited TED Talk. Complete the notes by filling in the missing words and drawing an arrow from the cause to the effect.

1. *sprmrkts sell 11cm pies* ———→ *apple pie* ————— *sales fall to 4th/5th*

2. *society will advance* ————————————— *= imprtnt tool*

3. *big data (BD)* ————————————————— *not do before*

4. *give data to mchn* ————————————— *signs of cancer*

5. ————————————————— *over time after temp period of dislocation*

J **TALK ABOUT CAUSAL RELATIONSHIPS** Think about how you would respond to the question "What effects has technology had on your life?" Make some notes about what you will say. Then follow the steps.

1. Find a partner and tell each other what effects one kind of technology has had on your lives.

2. Interview two other classmates on this topic. Take notes in the chart below during the interviews.

3. Work with your partner from step 1. Use your notes to summarize the interviews for your partner. Then listen to your partner's summaries.

Effects of One Kind of Technology on Life

Interview 1   Name: _____

Kind of technology	Effects

Interview 2   Name: _____

Kind of technology	Effects

K ▶ **1.23** **EXPAND YOUR VOCABULARY** Watch the excerpts from the TED Talk. Guess the meanings of the phrases in the box.

> | be sick of | burnt to a crisp | in this respect |
> | telltale signs | assembly line | frame of reference |

L **WATCH MORE** Go to TED.com to watch the full TED Talk by Kenneth Cukier.

AFTER YOU WATCH

M **THINK CRITICALLY** Categorize. Work with a partner. Look at the graphic. Match the four concepts to the correct definitions below.

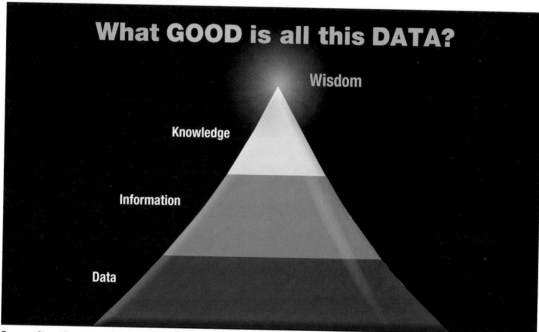

Source: Cloud Tweaks

_____ = raw, unanalyzed facts. There are more than 8 zettabytes of data stored worldwide today. That's 8 followed by 21 zeroes. You would need around 7.5 billion personal computers to store that much data.

_____ = the effective use of knowledge; decisions based on wisdom make good use of data.

_____ = understanding based on information; currently, just 0.5% of available information is analyzed.

_____ = value extracted from data; an estimated 33% of information could be useful if appropriately analyzed.

N **COMMUNICATE** Work in a small group. Discuss these questions.

1. It is estimated that there will be 40 zettabytes stored by 2020. In what ways is it a good thing that humans generate more data every year? In what ways is it not?

2. Do you think humans will learn more effective ways to turn knowledge into wisdom? Why and how, or why not?

O THINK CRITICALLY Interpret an Infographic. Work with a partner. Look at the infographic below. Write T if these statements about the infographic are *True*, F if they are *False*, or N if they are *Not mentioned*. Correct the false statements so they are true.

1. _____ Half of all data will be produced by people from just two countries.

2. _____ The amount of data produced in China and the United States will be roughly equal.

3. _____ India will produce just over half of the data produced by Western Europe.

4. _____ Asian countries will produce more data than countries in the Americas or Europe.

5. _____ China and the United States will produce more data than the rest of the world combined.

6. _____ India will produce more data than any single country in Western Europe.

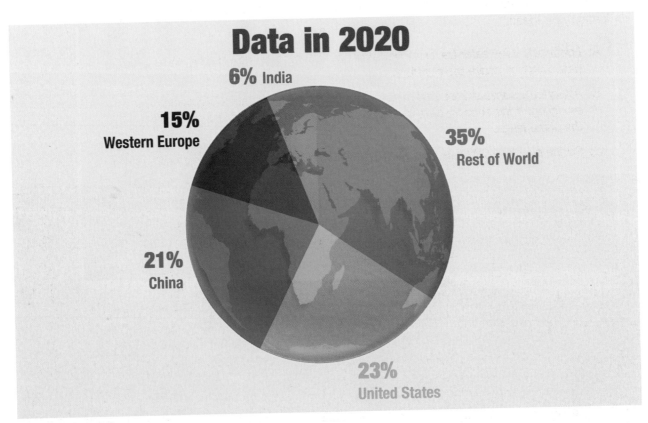

Data in 2020

6% India

15% Western Europe

35% Rest of World

21% China

23% United States

Source: SAS Institute, Inc.

Put It Together

A THINK CRITICALLY Synthesize. Work in a small group. Read the idea worth spreading from Cukier's TED Talk below. Then discuss the questions.

> Kenneth Cukier's idea worth spreading is that having more data allows us to see things more accurately and will help us solve the world's biggest problems.

1. What examples does Cukier give that illustrate how having more data allows us to see things more accurately?

2. What examples does Cukier give that illustrate how having more data might help us solve the world's biggest problems?

3. Does Cukier's idea worth spreading also apply to the main idea of the lecture in Part 1? If not, what is the lecture's main idea and how does it relate to big data?

B COMMUNICATE Work in a small group. What are some problems—global, local, or personal—that you would like to solve? How could having more data help? Discuss your ideas.

A: *I definitely think safer travel is important, but I'm not sure how having more data would improve travel safety.*

B: *Apparently some airlines use hundreds of sensors to get data while planes are flying. If the sensors detect a small issue, the airline can fix it as soon as the plane lands.*

C: *So the problem gets fixed before it becomes a serious issue? That's great!*

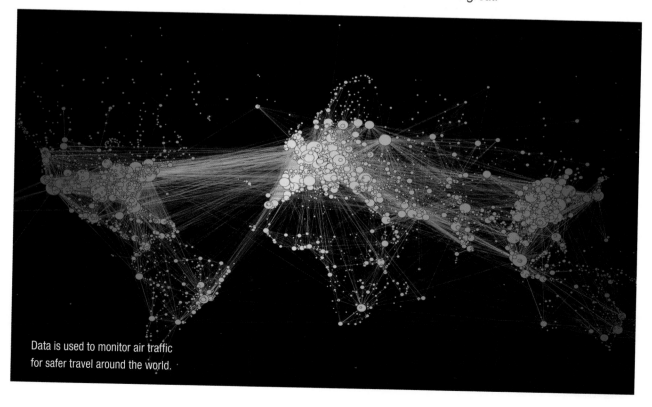

Data is used to monitor air traffic for safer travel around the world.

COMMUNICATE

ASSIGNMENT: Give a Pair Presentation With a partner, you will research and present an example of how big data has helped solve a problem or improve a situation. Review the ideas in Parts 1 and 2 and the listening and speaking skills as you prepare your presentation.

PREPARE

PRESENTATION SKILL Follow a Clear Organization

A good presentation should be easy for listeners to understand. One way to achieve this is to use a clear, logical organization for your talk. Here are some of the most common ways to organize a talk:

- **Chronological**—discuss ideas in the order in which they occurred
- **Topical**—talk about different aspects of the same topic or idea
- **Problem-solution**—discuss problems and their possible solutions
- **Cause-effect**—talk about the causes of a situation and their effects

You should choose the organization that is most suitable for your topic. You can help your listeners follow the organization by using transition phrases to signpost each point in your talk. For example, if your talk has a chronological organization, you could introduce each point with phrases like *First, Secondly, Then,* and so on.

C THINK CRITICALLY Analyze. Work in a small group. Look at the organization of Cukier's talk. Discuss which of the patterns in the skill box best describes it.

"Big Data is Better Data" by Kenneth Cukier

- Introduction to how and why big data is important
- Discussion of the ways society stores and uses data
- Overview of machine learning and its value to society
- Discussion of some of the drawbacks of big data
- Summary of the ways big data will change society

D **COLLABORATE** Work with your partner. Think of a problem that has been solved or a situation that could be improved by using big data. There are some sample topics with research notes on page 178. You can either use one of those or research your own idea as the basis for a presentation. (Even if you research your own topic, these examples will help you understand what information you need to find.) These questions may help you organize your presentation:

- What is the problem or situation?
- What kinds of data about it are available?
- How did or could big data help improve it?

E **COLLABORATE** Work with your partner. Take turns rehearsing your presentation. After each turn, give each other feedback about how to improve, especially in terms of having a clear, logical organization and explaining causal relationships clearly.

F Read the rubric on page 180 before you present. Notice how your presentation will be evaluated. Keep these categories in mind as you present and watch your classmates' presentations.

PRESENT

G Give your presentation to the class. Watch your classmates' presentations and listen carefully to how each person used data or information.

H **THINK CRITICALLY** Evaluate. Work in a small group. Share feedback on the presentations you watched and listen to feedback about yours. Tell the people in your group two things you liked and two things you will do better next time you make a presentation.

REFLECT

Reflect on what you have learned. Check [✓] your progress.

I can
☐ listen for and distinguish between facts and opinions.
☐ introduce causal relationships in three different ways.
☐ recognize and use the correct stress for compound nouns.
☐ note causal relationships when a speaker discusses them.
☐ choose and follow a clear, logical organization for presentations.

I understand the meanings of these words and can use them.
Circle those you know. Underline those you need to work on.

branch	eliminate AWL	notable	sector AWL
commerce	formula AWL	overlook	static
customize	hype	process AWL	store
demographic	labor AWL	prosper	trait
dynamic AWL	log	revolutionary AWL	transmit AWL

UNIT 5
Fear Factor

A man faces his fear of heights to capture the view above the city of Dubai.

THINK AND DISCUSS

1 Look at the photo and read the caption. Would you describe the man's actions as brave, foolish, or something else? Why? Would you do what he is doing? Why, or why not?

2 Fear of heights is a common fear. What effects do our fears—either common or uncommon ones—have on us?

BEFORE YOU LISTEN

A COMMUNICATE Work with a partner. Discuss these questions.

1. What are the main forms of media that people use these days?

2. Look at the image. How does it relate to the idea of fear in the media?

B COMMUNICATE You are going to listen to an academic discussion about how and why media stories often focus on fears that people have. Before you listen, discuss these questions in a small group.

1. What types of stories that focus on fears do you often see in the media?

2. Have you ever been affected after reading, viewing, or hearing such stories? If yes, why and how? If no, why not?

3. In your experience, do media stories often make situations sound worse than they really are? Support your opinion.

AS-13

VOCABULARY

C ⌂ 2.2 Read and listen to the paragraphs below with words from the academic discussion. Choose the best definition for each bold word.

a. Reports indicate that efforts to control the **epidemic** are working, and the number of new cases has gone down. The disease still **poses a risk,** however, and people traveling to the affected area should postpone their trips.

b. A storm warning is in effect for the East Beach area. If the forecast is **trustworthy,** the storm will arrive early on Saturday morning and will **generate** powerful winds. Local residents expressed **anxiety** about the potential damage to their homes.

c. Will a new self-help book let us **conquer** our fears? According to a **claim** by the publisher, readers will learn a basic **principle** for managing their fears. Is that claim **credible?** Well, the book includes many **anecdotes** from people who apparently overcame their fears by following the book's advice.

1. _Trustworthy_ (adj) able to be trusted or relied on

2. _Credible_ (adj) believable and convincing

3. _Epidemic_ (n) a disease that spreads quickly among many people

4. _Anxiety_ (n) a feeling of worry about what might happen

5. _principle_ (n) a rule or belief that guides how one behaves

6. _Anecdotes_ (n) short stories, often about one's personal experiences

7. _Claim_ (n) a statement saying that something is true

8. _poses a risk_ (v) represents a danger

9. _conquer_ (v) defeat or overcome something

10. _generate_ (v) produce or create something

D **COMMUNICATE** Work with a partner. Take turns answering these questions. Use the words in bold in your answers.

1. A good **principle** for life is to be kind to others. What is one principle you try to follow in your life?

2. Do you think media stories are more or less **trustworthy** than they used to be? Support your view.

3. Some people say that modern life is stressful. Would you make this **claim?** Why, or why not?

4. What are some things that **pose a risk** to your happiness? How could you avoid them?

5. Most people see **anxiety** as negative. Are there any positives to this feeling? Explain your answer.

6. What is one thing you want to **conquer?** How could you go about conquering it?

LISTEN

E **2.3** **LISTEN FOR MAIN IDEAS** Read the opinions below. Then listen to an academic discussion between a professor and two students in a seminar class. Write the name of the student who gave each opinion in the space: Mina (the female student), Mateo (the male student), or both.

OPINIONS	STUDENT
• There are more fear-based stories in the media than before.	
• The world is actually safer than it used to be.	
• The media focus on stories about people's fears to make money.	
• Media stories about fear can change people's behavior.	
• The world is more dangerous than it used to be.	

NOTE-TAKING SKILL Use Abbreviations for Numerical Details

It is often important to note numbers, dates, or other specific numerical details that you hear. You can take notes more quickly if you abbreviate these details. Here are some abbreviations you can use:

- fractions for numbers: *twenty-five percent: 1/4; one-third: 1/3; seven out of ten: 7/10*

- letters for large numbers: *thousand: K; million: M; billion: B*

- math symbols for common phrases: *less than: < ; more than: > ; approximately: ≈*

F **2.4** **LISTEN FOR DETAILS** Listen to segment 1 and take notes about the numerical details you hear. Then use your notes to add an abbreviation and/or a number to each statement.

1. Apparently, up to _____ of stories on local television news in the U.S. are about crime.

2. Although murder rates fell 20%, the number of media stories about it rose _____ %.

3. Steven Pinker's book *The Better Angels of Our Nature* has _____ pages.

4. In his book, Pinker says violent acts in schools have declined _____ % since the 1990s.

5. Pinker also says that in the last 15 years, murder rates have gone down in _____ of countries for which there is trustworthy data.

6. The female student argues that a media story with _____ views can generate more money from advertising than a less popular story.

Recognize Repetition

Speakers often repeat important information when they give a presentation. This can be their opinion, a key supporting detail, or a summary of a main idea.

Generally, a speaker does not repeat information using all of the same words. Instead, she will repeat information by paraphrasing what she said previously. Sometimes, she will introduce repeated information with a specific phrase such as "As I mentioned," "Like I said," or "In sum."

These days, I think that people are more frightened than ever before. . . . Like I said, in my view, people are more scared now than they were in the past.

G ∩ 2.5 **COMMUNICATE** Work with a partner. Listen to segment 2. Then answer the questions. When you have finished, compare your answers with another pair of students.

1. Which idea does the male student repeat three times?

2. Which phrase does the student use to introduce the final repetition of this idea?

3. Why do you think he repeats this idea three times?

AFTER YOU LISTEN

H THINK CRITICALLY Interpret an Infographic. Work in small groups. Match each example below to one of the "Domains of Fear" shown in the infographic. Answers may vary. Then think of one more example that matches each category.

DOMAIN	EXAMPLE 1	EXAMPLE 2
relationships	being lonely	
	climate change	
	getting fired	
	identity theft	
	losing data files	
	major storms	
	spiders or snakes	
	being unstylish	

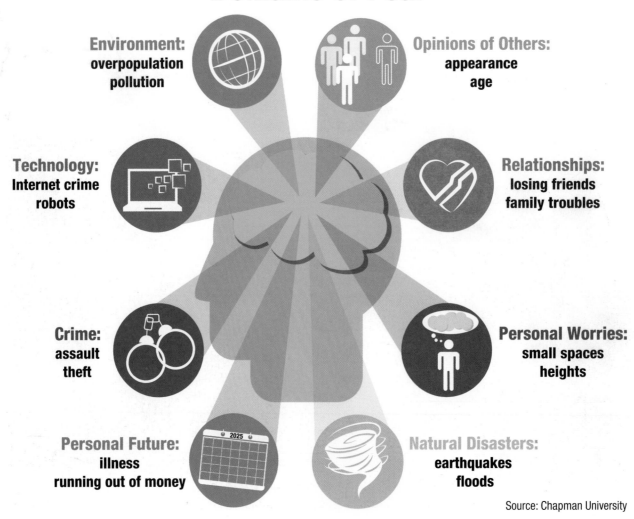

Domains of Fear

Environment: overpopulation pollution

Opinions of Others: appearance age

Technology: Internet crime robots

Relationships: losing friends family troubles

Crime: assault theft

Personal Worries: small spaces heights

Personal Future: illness running out of money

Natural Disasters: earthquakes floods

Source: Chapman University

I **COMMUNICATE** Add two of your own questions below. Interview a student in your class. Then share your results with a partner.

QUESTION	ANSWER
1. Which of the domains of fear impacts you the most?	
2. What do people in your country tend to worry about?	
3. Do you know anyone who is afraid of heights? (Who?)	
4. Do you worry more about pollution, overpopulation, or climate change?	
5. What is your number-one worry about technology?	
6. What natural disaster most frightens you?	
7.	
8.	

J **THINK CRITICALLY** **Personalize.** Work with a partner. Discuss these questions.

1. We are all afraid of something. What are some common things that people fear?
2. Why do people fear these things? What can they do to reduce their fears?

People are encouraged to handle a western hognose during a workshop to overcome their fear of snakes.

SPEAKING

Ask Questions

Speakers sometimes ask questions that act as "signposts" to help listeners follow their ideas. Specifically, speakers can use questions to:

1. Signal that they will define something

> Example: *Who knows what fear-based coverage is?*
> *So, what is fear-based coverage?*

2. Introduce a key idea or opinion

> Example: *Who thinks it's worse now?*
> *Some say it's worse now, but is this really true?*

3. Engage listeners by interacting with them or by suggesting that they share similar views

> Example: *Has anyone seen this before?*
> *We've all seen this before, haven't we?*

Here are some guidelines for asking questions:

- Keep your questions simple so that your listeners can easily understand them.

- Have a reason for each question you ask (and do not ask too many questions).

- Know what response you expect from listeners.

K **⌂ 2.6** Read these questions from the seminar discussion. Listen to segment 3, which includes excerpts from the discussion. Write the excerpt number next to the question(s) you hear. Then work with a partner. Discuss why the speaker uses each of these questions.

1. *"Haven't we all known people who got scared after seeing a story in the media?"*   Excerpt _____

2. *"Is that part of it?"* and *"Is it the whole story?"*   Excerpt _____

3. *"So, why is this happening?"* and *"Does the data support this argument, though?"*   Excerpt _____

4. *"We learned about 'if it bleeds, it leads,' right?"*   Excerpt _____

5. *"Why are there more fear-based stories?"*   Excerpt _____

PRONUNCIATION SKILL Thought Groups

Good speakers help listeners understand their words by speaking in "thought groups." A thought group is a phrase that expresses a single idea. At the end of each group, speakers slightly stress the last content word—called the "focus word"—and then briefly pause before continuing.

There is no rule for how to break a sentence into thought groups; however, sentences with too many or too few thought groups are often difficult for listeners to understand. Sentences that are divided at unnatural places can also be hard to understand. Listen to these examples.

∩ 2.7

Natural thought groups: *Think about it. // Just this year we've experienced // two natural disasters, // one major epidemic, // and more than the usual number of violent crimes.*

Unnatural thought groups: *Think about it. Just this year we've // experienced two natural // disasters, one major // epidemic, and more than the usual // number of violent crimes.*

(See page 172 in the *Independent Student Handbook* for more information about thought groups and pronunciation.)

L ∩ 2.8 COMMUNICATE Work with a partner. Look at the examples, which show different ways to divide a sentence into thought groups. Discuss whether you think each one would sound natural or unnatural, and why. Then listen and check.

1. Studies // show that // most people // have at least one // phobia.

2. Studies show // that most people // have at least one phobia.

3. Studies show that most people // have at least one phobia.

4. Studies show that // most people have at least one // phobia.

5. Studies show // that most people have at least one phobia.

M Practice reading this information aloud. Pause at the end of each thought group and stress the primary syllable of the underlined focus word.

A *phobia* can be <u>defined</u> // as a <u>strong</u>, // <u>lasting</u>, // and often irrational <u>fear</u>. //
Studies show that most <u>people</u> // have at least one <u>phobia</u>. //
Some of the most common <u>phobias</u> // include fear of <u>spiders</u>, // <u>snakes</u>, // and <u>heights</u>. //
Scientists are unsure why people develop <u>phobias</u>, // but one <u>theory</u> // is negative past <u>experiences</u>. //
Phobias can be hard to <u>conquer</u>, // but behavior therapy is sometimes an effective <u>treatment</u>.

What fear can teach us

❝ Fears and storytelling have the same components. **❞**

BEFORE YOU WATCH

A **COMMUNICATE** Read the title of the TED Talk and the information about Karen Thompson Walker. Think of something you fear. Does this fear cause you to imagine things? Discuss in small groups.

KAREN THOMPSON WALKER Novelist

Karen Thompson Walker is a writer. Her first novel, *The Age of Miracles,* was published in 2012. It tells the story of an unusual natural disaster that affects the whole world: Earth goes around the sun more and more slowly, and days get longer and longer. The story describes people's hopes and fears as well as the emotional, physical, and social effects of the disaster.

Karen Thompson Walker's idea worth spreading is that if we understand how fear stimulates our imaginations, we can benefit by preparing for what might happen in the future.

What makes a bad presenter? → 95

B **COMMUNICATE** Work in small groups. Discuss the following questions.

1. Read the quote. What are some fears that authors often depict in stories? How might fears and stories be connected?

2. Talk about a time when you were scared. Did you learn anything from that fear? Why, or why not?

3. What other emotions, such as happiness or anger, can also teach us something? Support your view.

VOCABULARY

C [🎧 2.9] These sentences will help you learn words in the TED Talk. Read and listen to the sentences. Then write the number of the sentence in which the bold word matches the definition.

1. Anne gave an **insightful** talk that clearly explained how people can overcome their deepest fears.

2. Jenny found it hard to believe all of the **rumors** about the epidemic, but they still frightened her.

3. Tom understood what it felt like to **starve** after being lost in a desert for a week without any food.

4. The guest speaker used powerful **imagery** that helped people understand and accept her ideas.

5. The novel, which had so much **suspense** that people could not stop reading it, became a bestseller.

6. Studies show that news stories about violent crimes often **provoke** a strong reaction in readers.

7. Audiences found the movie very frightening, even though most of the scary moments were **subtle.**

8. As soon as news of the disaster spread, volunteers rushed to the hospital to help the **survivors.**

9. Zack's **dread** of both heights and wide-open spaces made it hard for him to live a normal life.

10. Sofia let her worries about the journey **influence** her decision about when and how to travel.

a. (v) affect somebody's opinion about something   Sentence _____

b. (v) cause a response or emotion, especially anger   Sentence _____

c. (n) a deep and powerful fear   Sentence _____

d. (n) excitement and uncertainty about what might happen   Sentence _____

e. (adj) able to see and explain the truth about something   Sentence _____

f. (adj) not direct, obvious, or easy to sense   Sentence _____

g. (n) people who remain alive after a deadly event   Sentence _____

h. (n) stories or gossip that may not be true   Sentence _____

i. (v) suffer or die from lack of food   Sentence _____

j. (adj) visually descriptive language   Sentence _____

D COMMUNICATE Work in small groups. Discuss the questions. Use the bold words in your answers.

1. Who is the most **insightful** person you know? Tell your group about this person.

2. What could you say to a friend to get him or her to stop spreading **rumors** about other people?

3. Describe a suspenseful moment from a movie you have seen. What gave this scene so much **suspense?**

4. Which of these would most likely **provoke** a reaction in you: seeing a photo of a spider, a snake, or a shark? What reaction would it provoke, and why?

5. Do you know anybody with a **dread** of something? How does it affect this person's behavior?

6. Do your worries or concerns often **influence** your behavior? Why and how, or why not?

WATCH

learnmore Herman Melville was an American writer who lived from 1819 to 1891. As a young man, he hunted whales on a whaleship. During this time, he visited the Marquesas Islands in the South Pacific Ocean near the island of Tahiti. Melville wrote a novel about his experiences called *Moby-Dick.* It tells the story of a ship's captain who hunts a white sperm whale that had previously destroyed his ship. *Moby-Dick* did not sell well at first, but many people now see it as a great novel.

WORDS IN THE TALK
cannibal (n): a person who eats another person
remote (adj): far away (from other places)
unintentional (adj): by mistake rather than on purpose
vivid (adj): easy to see or producing strong images in the mind

E ▶ **1.24** **WATCH FOR MAIN IDEAS** Watch segment 1 of the TED Talk. Which of the two statements below is the speaker's main goal? Why do you think so? Discuss with a partner.

- Her main goal is to tell the amazing and little-known story of the men of the whaleship *Essex*.

- Her main goal is to illustrate an idea about fear by describing what the men of the *Essex* experienced.

F ▶ **1.25** **COMMUNICATE** Watch the rest of the edited TED Talk. Do you still hold the same opinion of Thompson Walker's goal? Why, or why not? Discuss with a different partner.

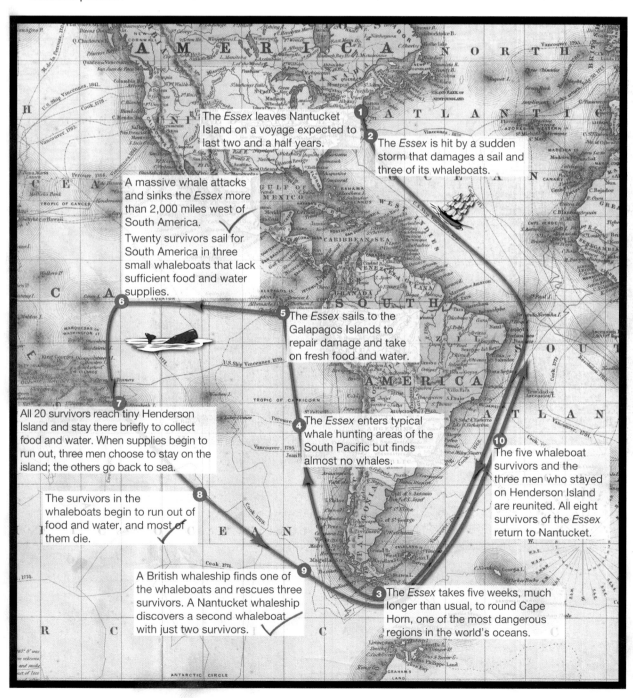

The *Essex* leaves Nantucket Island on a voyage expected to last two and a half years.

The *Essex* is hit by a sudden storm that damages a sail and three of its whaleboats.

A massive whale attacks and sinks the *Essex* more than 2,000 miles west of South America.

Twenty survivors sail for South America in three small whaleboats that lack sufficient food and water supplies.

The *Essex* sails to the Galapagos Islands to repair damage and take on fresh food and water.

All 20 survivors reach tiny Henderson Island and stay there briefly to collect food and water. When supplies begin to run out, three men choose to stay on the island; the others go back to sea.

The *Essex* enters typical whale hunting areas of the South Pacific but finds almost no whales.

The five whaleboat survivors and the three men who stayed on Henderson Island are reunited. All eight survivors of the *Essex* return to Nantucket.

The survivors in the whaleboats begin to run out of food and water, and most of them die.

A British whaleship finds one of the whaleboats and rescues three survivors. A Nantucket whaleship discovers a second whaleboat with just two survivors.

The *Essex* takes five weeks, much longer than usual, to round Cape Horn, one of the most dangerous regions in the world's oceans.

G ▶ **1.26** **WATCH FOR DETAILS** Look at the map on page 95 showing what happened to the whaleship *Essex*. Watch the video again. Which three of the events shown on the map does Thompson Walker mention?

H **THINK CRITICALLY** Infer. Work with a partner. Compare your answers to exercise G. Then choose two of the events shown on the map that Thomspon Walker did not mention. Why do you think she chose not to talk about these two events?

I ▶ **1.27** **RECOGNIZE REPETITION** Watch segment 3 of the talk. Which four of these ideas does Thompson Walker repeat?

   a. The idea that English speakers see fear as something to conquer

   b. The various dangers that were faced by the men of the *Essex*

   c. The rumors that were heard by the men of the *Essex*

   d. How fears are similar to stories in some ways

   e. The ways in which our fears make us consider the future

   f. How some entrepreneurs pay close attention to their fears

J **ASK QUESTIONS** Work with a partner. Underline the questions in these excerpts. Then come up with a way to simplify or restate each question. Take turns saying each excerpt with the original question and then with your new question.

   1. *"In English, fear is something we conquer. It's something we fight. It's something we overcome. But what if we looked at fear in a fresh way? What if we thought of fear as an amazing act of the imagination, something that can be as profound and insightful as storytelling itself?"*

   2. *"Now we might just as easily call these fears by a different name. What if instead of calling them fears, we called them stories? Because that's really what fear is, if you think about it."*

   3. *"Once in a while, our fears can predict the future. But we can't possibly prepare for all of the fears that our imaginations concoct. So how can we tell the difference between the fears worth listening to and all the others?"*

   4. *"So the question is, why did these men dread cannibals so much more than the extreme likelihood of starvation? Why were they swayed by one story so much more than the other?"*

K THINK CRITICALLY Evaluate. Work with a different partner. Look again at the questions in the excerpts in exercise J. Discuss these questions.

1. Which of the questions that Thompson Walker asks

   - signal that she will define something? *2*
   - introduce a key idea or opinion? *2 43*
   - engage her listeners? *1*

2. Rewrite the questions in exercise J as statements. Say each excerpt with the original question. Then say it with the rewritten statement. Which version sounds better in your view? Why?

L ▶ 1.28 EXPAND YOUR VOCABULARY Watch the excerpts from the TED Talk. Guess the meanings of the phrases in the box.

dire situation	dismiss one's fears	illuminating example
embark on	resort to	steer for

M WATCH MORE Go to TED.com to watch the full TED Talk by Karen Thompson Walker.

AFTER YOU WATCH

N THINK CRITICALLY Infer. Look back at the map on page 95. Thompson Walker says that fears are like stories we tell ourselves about the future. What fears do you think the people below might have had, and what stories might they have told themselves about the future? Discuss in small groups.

> A: *I bet the families were scared that some of the men of the* Essex *might not come home.*
>
> B: *Yes, but they probably told themselves that everything would be OK in the end.*

1. The families of the men on the *Essex* when the ship left Nantucket on its voyage

2. The men of the *Essex* when they realized that a whale was attacking their ship

3. The three men who chose to stay on Henderson Island although it had little food and water

4. People living in Nantucket when the eight survivors of the *Essex* returned home

O THINK CRITICALLY Personalize. Work in small groups. Think about a journey you have taken. Then take turns sharing your answers to these questions.

1. What fear(s) did you have before the journey? Why?

2. What fear(s) did you have in the middle of the journey? Why?

3. How closely did your fears predict what actually happened?

P THINK CRITICALLY Interpret. Thích Nhất Hạnh is a peace activist, teacher, and writer from Vietnam. Read the quote. To what extent do you think Karen Thompson Walker would agree with his idea about fear? Why? What do you think of his idea? Share your views with the class.

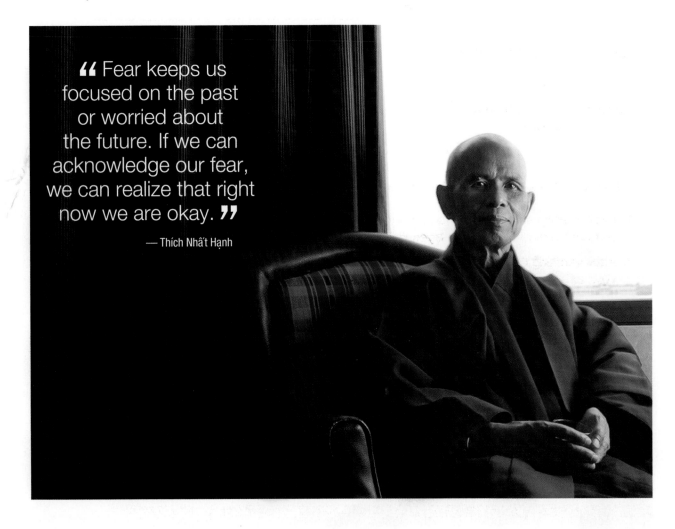

❝ Fear keeps us focused on the past or worried about the future. If we can acknowledge our fear, we can realize that right now we are okay. ❞

— Thích Nhất Hạnh

Put It Together

A **THINK CRITICALLY** Synthesize. Work with a partner. Complete the table by summarizing information from the seminar discussion in Part 1 and the TED Talk in Part 2. Write at least one piece of information in each blank cell. When you have finished, share your ideas with another pair of students.

	SEMINAR DISCUSSION: FEAR IN THE MEDIA	TED TALK: WHAT FEAR CAN TEACH US
Key idea expressed about fear	*Media stories about people's fears attract readers or viewers.*	
Examples of people's fears		
Examples of fear affecting people's behavior		

B **THINK CRITICALLY** Reflect. Work in small groups. Discuss these questions.

1. After listening to the seminar discussion, will you look at media stories about fears differently in the future? If yes, how? If no, why not?

2. After watching the TED Talk, will you deal with your fears in a different way? Why, or why not?

COMMUNICATE

ASSIGNMENT: Give an Individual Presentation You will give a presentation about how an emotion—such as fear, love, anger, or happiness—can teach us something useful. Illustrate your overall message with a personal story. Review the ideas in Parts 1 and 2 and the listening and speaking skills as you prepare your presentation.

PREPARE

Telling a story—either about something that happened to you personally or about something you heard—is often an interesting way to support your message. There are three common ways to use a story in a talk or presentation:

1. Tell the story first. Then give the overall message and explain how the story is relevant to it.

2. Give the overall message first. Then give the story as an example to support the message.

3. Break the story and overall message into parts. Say part of the story and then part of the message. Repeat in this way so that the story and message are woven together.

C THINK CRITICALLY Analyze. Work in small groups. Discuss these questions.

1. Which of the three approaches to telling a story mentioned in the skill box above does Mina, the female student, use in the seminar discussion?

2. Which approach does Karen Thompson Walker use in her TED Talk? Would you have chosen the same approach? Why, or why not?

3. Which approach do you think is easiest for a speaker to use? Why? Is this approach also the easiest for listeners? Why, or why not?

D COLLABORATE Write a presentation outline in note form. Use these questions as a guide. Then share your notes with a partner. Help each other improve your notes by asking questions and giving feedback.

Your Overall Message

What emotion will you talk about? _____

What can this emotion teach us? _____

Your Story

Who did this story happen to? _____

When and where did this story happen? _____

What are the main events of the story? _____

_____

How does the story illustrate your overall message? _____

_____

E Revise your presentation outline based on feedback from your partner in Exercise D. Then practice your presentation several times. As you practice, remember to stress the primary syllable of the last content word of each thought group and then pause slightly after each thought group.

F Read the rubric on page 181. Notice how your presentation will be evaluated. Keep these categories in mind as you present and watch your classmates' presentations.

PRESENT

G Give your presentation to the class. Watch your classmates' presentations. After you watch each one, provide feedback using the rubric as a guide. Add notes or any other feedback you want to share.

H **THINK CRITICALLY** Evaluate. Work in a small group. Share feedback on the presentations you watched and listen to feedback about your presentation. Tell the people in your group whether you were satisfied with your presentation. Say why, or why not.

REFLECT

Reflect on what you have learned. Check [✓] your progress.

I can
- [ ] use symbols and abbreviations to make note of numerical details.
- [ ] listen for repetition and understand the speaker's purpose in using it.
- [ ] ask questions when I am speaking.
- [ ] speak in thought groups, stressing the focus word and then pausing.
- [ ] use stories to support my ideas when I am making a presentation.

I understand the meanings of these words and can use them.
Circle those you know. Underline those you need to work on.

anecdote	dread	insightful AWL	starve
anxiety	epidemic	pose a risk	subtle
claim	generate AWL	principle AWL	survivor AWL
conquer	imagery AWL	provoke	suspense
credible	influence	rumors	trustworthy

Food for Thought

Farmed juvenile glass eels are sold to fish farmers in Asia who will raise them for sale in fish markets. The population of wild eels has declined in the U.S. in the past decade, prompting the federal government to consider listing the species as threatened.

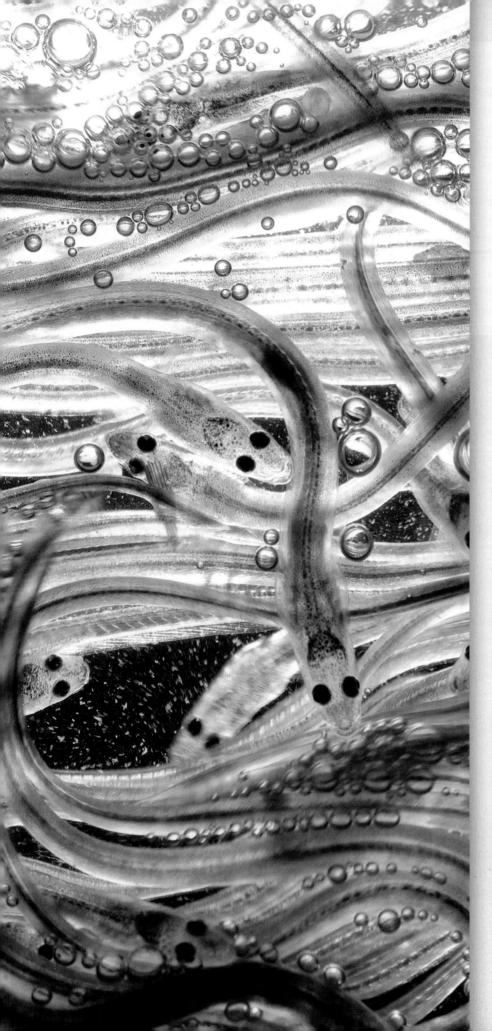

THINK AND DISCUSS

1 Look at the photo and read the caption. Would you be willing to eat eels, whether farmed or wild? Why, or why not?

2 The phrase "food for thought" is used when discussing something that makes one think seriously about an issue. Share a time when you learned about something that gave you "food for thought."

BEFORE YOU LISTEN

A COMMUNICATE Work with a partner. Discuss these questions.

1. Look at the photo and read the caption. How do you feel about eating genetically altered foods?

2. Think about what your grandparents ate and how they prepared it. In what ways has technology changed how we prepare food and what we eat?

3. Science fiction often shows food being produced instantly by machines. Would you be happy to eat food produced in this way? Why, or why not?

B ⌂ 2.10 COMMUNICATE Work in a small group. Complete the tasks.

1. You are going to hear a discussion in an environmental science class. The professor begins by talking about "the food crisis." A *crisis* is an emergency. What do you know, or what can you imagine, about this crisis? Discuss.

2. The professor asks her students to research how technology might solve the food crisis. In general, do you believe that technology can solve big problems like this? Discuss.

3. Listen to segment 1 of the discussion. Does the professor's explanation of the food crisis match your ideas? Does the professor's view about technology match your views? Discuss.

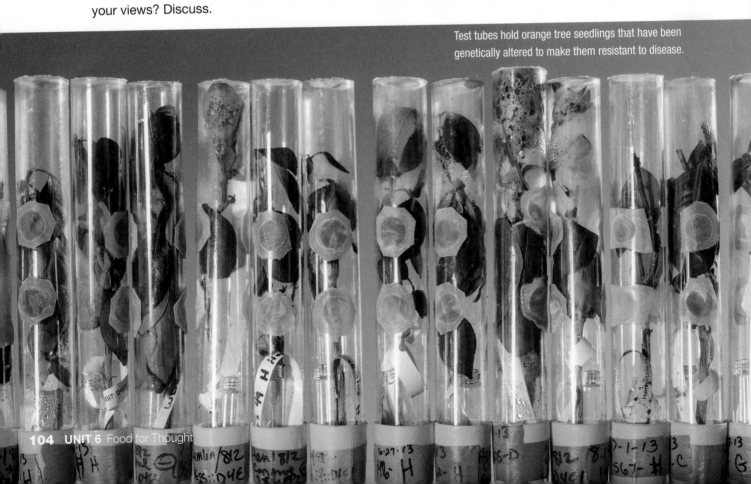

Test tubes hold orange tree seedlings that have been genetically altered to make them resistant to disease.

VOCABULARY

C [2.11] Read and listen to these paragraphs with words from the discussion. Then complete each definition with one of the bold words.

a. Some kinds of shellfish, including clams, mussels, and oysters, can **filter** pollution from the water in which they live. This ability to remove pollutants means they play an important **ecological** role.

b. One study suggests consumers may **discard** up to one quarter of the food they buy. Some people are **skeptical** whether the real figure is this high, but others believe it and have taken steps to reduce their food waste. Still others take a **neutral** position and say that more studies need to be conducted.

c. Some chefs are famous for using unusual **ingredients** in their recipes, including fruits and vegetables that are **edible** but rarely eaten. In addition to being delicious, these unusual foods are often rich in **nutrients.**

d. Farmed fish used to be a **niche** product, but it now makes up around 40 percent of the fish purchased in some countries. This increase comes at a cost, though, as **conventional** aquaculture, or fish farming, can cause pollution.

1. _____ (adj) related to the connections among plants, animals, and people

2. _____ (adj) not supporting any position or side in an argument

3. _____ (n) the foods and substances that are used to make a particular dish

4. _____ (n) substances in food, such as vitamins, that are necessary for life

5. _____ (adj) related to products or services that are for a limited market or group

6. _____ (v) remove something that is unwanted from a liquid or gas

7. _____ (v) throw away something that is unwanted or not useful

8. _____ (adj) usual or traditional

9. _____ (adj) doubtful or disbelieving

10. _____ (adj) can be eaten

D **COMMUNICATE** Work with a partner. Take turns responding to these questions. Use the bold words in your responses.

1. What is one issue that you are **neutral** about? Explain why you do not support one side or another.

2. What **ingredients** are needed to make your favorite dish? Where can you buy them?

3. What are some foods with a lot of **nutrients** that you enjoy eating? How often do you eat them?

4. Would you agree or disagree that, these days, people often **discard** things that still have value? Why?

5. Think of a time when you chose not to act in a **conventional** way. What did you do, and why?

6. What is the most unusual **edible** thing you have ever eaten? When, where, and why did you eat it?

LISTEN

E 🎧 **2.12** ▶ **1.29** **LISTEN FOR MAIN IDEAS** Listen to segment 2 of the discussion. Then match these main ideas to the person who says them. One answer matches both people, and two answers won't be used.

    a. Aquaponics combines two ways of farming into one.

    b. Conventional farming lacks the benefits of aquaponics.

    c. Technology has already benefited many who lack food.

    d. There are various possible solutions to the food crisis.

    e. Traditional methods of farming result in polluted water.

    f. Using 3D printers is not likely to solve the food crisis.

The professor: __F__ __d__   The female student: __F__ __A__ __B__

F 🎧 **2.13** **LISTEN FOR DETAILS** Work with a partner. Complete the summaries of the two kinds of food technology discussed by adding the correct word to each blank. Use two words twice. Then listen to segment 3 to check your answers.

> farms   layers   nutrients
> items   machines   plants

3D food printers work by printing __layers__ of powdered ingredients on top of each other. These build up to produce __items__ of food. In the future, they might be able to add __nutrients__ to foods, but currently the __machines__ are slow, costly, and only suitable for non-essential foods.

Aquaponics __farms__ produce both crops and fish. They have two __layers__. On top are the crops growing in water that is rich in __nutrients__. On the bottom are tanks of fish. The fish produce waste. This waste is added to the water in which the __plants__ grow.

WORDS IN THE DISCUSSION

cell (n): the basic unit that makes up plants and animals
protein (n): a substance found in meat or fish that is necessary in people's diets
soil (n): the top layers of earth in which plants grow

LISTENING SKILL Ask Questions

Asking questions before, during, and after listening can help you listen effectively.

1. Before listening, think of questions about the topic. Then listen for the answers to your questions while the speaker is talking. For example, if the topic is fish farms, your questions might include:

   What is the speaker's opinion about fish farms?
   Do fish farms produce high-quality fish?

2. While listening, think of questions about things you would like to know more about and write them down. If possible, ask the speaker your questions when he or she finishes. Your questions might include:

   What other fish species are suitable for fish farming?
   What is the environmental impact of fish farming?

3. After listening, review your notes and memory of what the speaker(s) said. If you think of more questions at this time, write them down. Then improve your understanding of the topic either by speaking to somebody who can answer your questions or researching the answers yourself.

G 🎧 2.14 ▶ 1.29 **COLLABORATE** Work in a small group. Complete the tasks.

1. You are going to listen to part of the discussion in which a student talks about a technology to grow meat. Before you listen, discuss and write down some questions about this topic.

2. Listen to segment 4. Write down any other questions that occur to you.

3. After listening, think about what you heard. Write down any other questions you would like to ask.

4. Share your questions with your group members. Discuss how you could find the answers.

Meat being grown in a lab

An expensive gourmet burger

H COMMUNICATE Work with a partner. Discuss these questions.

1. For you, when is the most effective time to write questions: before, during, or after listening? Why?

2. How soon after listening is the best time to review your notes and write additional questions? Why?

NOTE-TAKING SKILL Note Who Says What

Sometimes you will have to take notes when several people are speaking or when one speaker quotes the words of others. In both cases, you should indicate who says what in your notes.

If you know that you will hear multiple speakers *before* you start taking notes, you can divide your notes into different sections for each speaker. If you do not know until *after* you start taking notes, you can add to your notes in the following ways:

- Write the name (first or last) or initials of the speaker—for example: *Mark, Zuckerberg,* or *MZ*

- If you don't know the speaker's name, you can abbreviate his or her job, role, or speaking order—for example: *prof* for *professor, int* for *interviewer,* or *S3* for *third speaker*

- You can also abbreviate the speaker's gender—for example: *M* or ♂ for *man,* or *W* or ♀ for *woman*

I COLLABORATE Work in a small group. Complete the tasks.

1. How likely are you to hear multiple speakers when listening in these situations? Write L for *likely* or U for *unlikely*.

_____ lecture		_____ podcast	
_____ seminar		_____ online video	
_____ meeting		_____ radio interview	
_____ debate		_____ presentation	

2. Write how you would abbreviate these speakers in your notes. Then compare your abbreviations with those of the other people in your group.

_____ student		_____ fish farming expert	
_____ lecturer		_____ second male speaker	
_____ radio announcer		_____ office manager	
_____ female presenter		_____ third employee	

J 🎧 **2.15 COMMUNICATE** Listen to segment 5. Complete the notes by adding the speakers. Then discuss with a partner what each abbreviation in the notes means and which other words you could abbreviate.

1. ___F Stv.___
   Amal

   AQ = less nrg / resources than conven farms   *(SfCS*

   companies developing LED lights = less nrg / no heat

   LEDs help crops grow well—e.g., sweet pots /

   straws / tomatoes

2. ___Prof___

   agree 3D prntng not obvious solutn to FC

3. ___Austin___
   Mstu

   technol to grow meat in lab = may be sustainable   *StbL.*

   solutn to FC

AFTER YOU LISTEN

K THINK CRITICALLY Evaluate. Work in a small group. Discuss these questions.

1. In what ways, if any, has the global food crisis affected your country?

2. Which of the three technologies discussed by the students is the most likely to solve the food crisis? Why do you think so?

3. What other technologies, such as fish farming, do you think might have an impact on the food crisis?

L COLLABORATE Work with a partner. Write some questions that you would like to ask the two students—Amal and Austin—about the topics they researched. Then discuss your questions with another pair of students.

Earthquake victims in Nepal receive emergency food and water.
Natural disasters can contribute to the global food crisis.

SPEAKING

(See page 166 in the *Independent Student Handbook* for more information about expressing your position.)

M COMMUNICATE Read these excerpts from the discussion. Underline the phrases the speakers use to state their positions. Then work with a partner and use the underlined phrases to state your own positions about the following topics: how to solve the food crisis, the importance of eating healthily, what foods parents should never give their children.

1. *"Personally, I'm neutral on the value of technology as a potential solution to the food crisis. For me, it's just one among several options."*

2. *"So I feel that printing food will be a niche technology at best, and I'd like to discuss aquaponics instead. . . . For me, it has great potential to provide healthy, sustainable food."*

3. *"At first, I was skeptical and didn't think the technology would be important. As I researched, though, I came to think it has a lot of potential as a sustainable solution to the food crisis."*

Aquaponics could offer one solution to the food crisis.

PRONUNCIATION SKILL Connected Speech

In normal connected speech, speakers link some sounds together and omit other sounds.

1. **Vowel–vowel linking:** Add a /w/ or /y/ sound to link a vowel sound at the end of one word with one at the start of the next word (e.g., *show about* /sho_wabout/).

2. **Consonant–vowel linking:** Hold the consonant sound at the end of one word so it links with a vowel sound at the start of the next word (e.g., *heard a* /hear_da/).

3. **Consonant–consonant linking:** Hold the consonant sound at the end of one word and link it to the next consonant if the next word starts with the same consonant sound (e.g., *about two* / about_two/).

4. **Elision:** If a word ends with an unstressed /t/ or /d/ consonant sound, you can omit the /t/ or /d/ sound (e.g., *student heard* /studen_heard/).

Listen to this example of connected speech, which demonstrates elision and the three kinds of linking:

🎧 **2.16**

The student heard a radio show about two solutions to the food crisis.

/The studen_hear_da radio sho_wabout_two solutions to the food crisis/

N 🎧 **2.17** Work with a partner. Decide which sounds will be linked and which sounds will be omitted in this excerpt. Then listen and check your answers. Finally, practice saying the excerpt with the correct linked and omitted sounds.

*"And aquaponics requires far less energy and resources than conventional farms.
I even read that companies are developing LED lightbulbs for this kind of farming."*

O COLLABORATE Work with a partner. Complete these tasks.

1. Predict some of the reasons why people would *not* eat one or both of these foods: a salad made with aquaponically grown vegetables and a burger made from laboratory-grown meat.

2. Interview other students and write down their answers and reasons.

3. Share the interview data with your partner. Were your predictions accurate?

NAME	EAT SALAD?	EAT BURGER?	REASONS (IF NO)

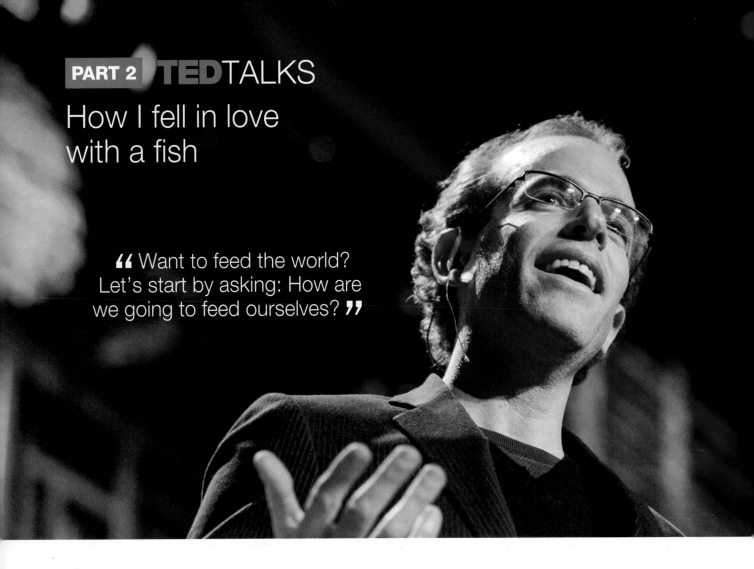

How I fell in love with a fish

❝ Want to feed the world? Let's start by asking: How are we going to feed ourselves? **❞**

BEFORE YOU WATCH

A COMMUNICATE Work in a small group. Read the title of the TED Talk and the information about Dan Barber. Then discuss the questions.

1. Barber is described as a "well-known chef." Who are some other well-known chefs? Are they only famous for their cooking abilities?

2. Barber's talk is about falling in love with a fish. What do you think he means by this, and why do you think he chose this title for his talk?

DAN BARBER   Chef

Dan Barber is a well-known chef who runs two restaurants in the New York City area. He has won multiple awards for the quality of his cooking. His restaurants serve food that has been grown locally or raised under sustainable conditions. Barber has written books and articles about how delicious food, healthy eating, and sustainable farming should all be connected.

Dan Barber's idea worth spreading is that if we adopt more sustainable food production methods, we can produce food that is good for the planet, good for us, and good to eat.

B COMMUNICATE Work with a partner. Do you think chefs usually have positive or negative views of aquaculture, or fish farming? Why? In his talk, Barber speaks very positively about *Veta la Palma,* a fish farm in Spain. Make a list of questions you have about this fish farm.

VOCABULARY

C ⌂ **2.18** These sentences will help you learn words in the edited TED Talk. Read and listen to the sentences. Then choose the answer that has the same meaning as each bold word.

1. The restaurant owner reviewed the plans and adopted the one that had the fewest **drawbacks.**
   a. disadvantages   b. opportunities   c. solutions

2. During cooking, the **conversion** of some substances into sugars adds delicious flavor to food.
   a. process   b. change   c. observation

3. Fish are often concentrated in schools, or groups, in nutrient-rich waters rather than being equally **distributed** across the oceans.
   a. caught up   b. spread out   c. stuck together

4. The chef was pleased to see that her customers were happily **feasting** on the dishes she prepared.
   a. making good choices   b. discussing in detail   c. eating large amounts

5. The organic market almost went out of business last year, but it is **thriving** under the new manager.
   a. having a hard time   b. doing very well   c. developing a little

6. The expert pointed out that much more food could be grown on the land if it were farmed **intensively** rather than extensively, as is currently the case.
   a. from time to time   b. with maximum effort   c. as a general rule

7. The villagers installed a filter to **purify** the water they were drinking and using for cooking.
   a. remove impurities from   b. remember the uses of   c. reduce the effects of

8. The book was popular because the author presented a clear **conception** of how to eat healthily.
   a. idea or understanding   b. option or decision   c. time or schedule

9. The chef was criticized for being an idealist, rather than a **realist,** about sustainable food production.
   a. person focusing on choices   b. person focusing on goals   c. person focusing on facts

10. The politician argued that the only way to restore the health of the oceans and avoid **depleting** fish stocks was to catch fewer fish.
    a. clearing up   b. keeping up   c. using up

D COMMUNICATE Work with a partner. Take turns responding to these questions. Use the bold words in your responses.

1. Winning the lottery is many people's dream. Are there any **drawbacks** to winning?

2. If you could choose several foods to **feast** on, which ones would you choose? Why?

3. Think of a **thriving** business, such as a restaurant, that you know. What are some reasons it is doing so well?

4. Have you ever done something **intensively**? What did you do and why? What was the result?

5. In general, are you more of a **realist** or the opposite, an idealist? Explain.

6. Name some daily tasks that **deplete** your energy level. What tasks recharge you?

WATCH

learn**more** *Veta la Palma* fish farm is located on an island in the Guadalquivir River. The river runs through southwestern Spain and empties into the Atlantic Ocean. The land was once used for beef cattle but is now used for aquaculture, or fish farming, as well as growing crops and raising animals. *Veta la Palma* is not a traditional fish farm in that its goals are not just to raise fish, but also to enhance the environmental quality of the area and generate new economic value in a sustainable way.

E ▶ **1.30 WATCH FOR MAIN IDEAS** Read these pairs of statements. Then watch the edited TED Talk. Check (✓) the statement in each pair that accurately summarizes one of Barber's main points.

1a. ___✓___ Chefs want to sell fish that is sustainable, but global fish stocks are declining.

1b. _____ Chefs are concerned because many species of fish are becoming hard to catch.

2a. _____ The goal of agriculture is to farm intensively so that farmers benefit rather than predators.

2b. ___✓___ The goal of agriculture, including fish farming, should be to create food that is delicious.

3a. ___✓___ Focusing on the relationships among plants and animals will lead to better food.

3b. _____ Focusing on how to feed communities will let farmers produce more food.

WORDS IN THE TALK
aquatic (adj): related to water
contaminants (n): substances that cause pollution; impurities
pesticides (n): substances used by farmers to control insects or other harmful organisms
plankton (n): tiny plants and animals that live in water
radical (adj): related to a change that would affect the traditional way of doing things

F ▶ **1.31** **WATCH FOR DETAILS** Watch segment 1. Check (✓) the points about *Veta la Palma* that Barber discusses. Then compare your answers with a partner.

1. ✓ Miguel, the biologist at *Veta la Palma*, is an expert in relationships, not in fish.

2. ✓ *Veta la Palma* does not feed its fish because they eat the same food as wild fish.

3. _____ Directors often film movies at *Veta la Palma* because it is such a beautiful place.

4. ✓ *Veta la Palma* loses one fifth of its fish and eggs to predators such as flamingos.

5. ✓ Miguel thinks that the number of birds at *Veta la Palma* shows the system's health.

6. ✓ The water at *Veta la Palma* comes from a polluted river, but the system purifies it.

G **COMMUNICATE** Work in a small group. Look at your list of questions from exercise B on page 113. Which of your questions were answered in the talk, and which ones are still unanswered?

H **ASK QUESTIONS** Work in a small group. Write some questions you would like to ask either Dan Barber or Miguel, the biologist at *Veta la Palma*. Then share your questions with another group. Decide on the five most important questions in your shared lists and discuss how you could find answers to them.

I ▶ **1.32** **NOTE WHO SAYS WHAT** Barber is the only speaker in his talk, but he quotes several other people. Take notes as you watch segment 2, which includes excerpts from the talk. Who does Barber quote? How did you indicate each speaker in your notes?

J ▶ **1.33** **WATCH FOR THE SPEAKER'S POSITION** Read the statements. Then watch segment 3. Indicate the order in which Barber gives his position on these issues by numbering the statements from 1 to 5.

_5_ Farmers who know about ecological relationships produce good food.

_4_ In order to feed the world, communities should first be able to feed themselves.

_2_ Small family farms and farmers' markets are worth supporting.

_3_ The future of good food will include produce that is locally grown and organic.

_1_ The goal of agriculture should be to produce delicious food.

K **THINK CRITICALLY** **Reflect.** Work in a small group. Take turns stating your position on each of the five issues listed in exercise J.

L ▶ **1.34** **EXPAND YOUR VOCABULARY** Watch the excerpts from the TED Talk. Guess the meanings of the phrases in the box.

> for better or for worse   a straight answer   set somebody up
> soak up   work its way through

M **WATCH MORE** Go to TED.com to watch the full TED Talk by Dan Barber.

An eco-tourism resort amid Maya ruins in Belize

AFTER YOU WATCH

N THINK CRITICALLY Reflect. Work in a small group. Discuss these questions.

1. After learning about the methods used there, would you like to eat fish from *Veta la Palma?* Why, or why not?

2. If you could go on an eco-vacation to *Veta la Palma,* would you like to go? Why, or why not?

3. Do you think *Veta la Palma* will become the new global standard for fish farms? Why, or why not?

O THINK CRITICALLY Interpret an Infographic. Work with a partner. Choose the word in parentheses that completes the sentence so that it correctly summarizes information from the top section of the infographic on page 118. Then compare your answers with another pair of students.

1. Between 2006 and 2008, human demand for fish increased by (*about* / *under*) five million tons.

2. In contrast, the world's supply of fish dropped (*slightly* / *substantially*) in the same period.

3. From 2008 to 2011, demand for fish rose from 119.7 million tons to (*almost* / *over*) 131 million tons.

4. In the same period, there was a further small decline in supply of (*around* / *up to*) half a million tons.

5. By the year 2030, demand for fish is expected to reach (*approximately* / *exactly*) 154 million tons.

DON PR   "So far out waste gets distributed" not concern."

DON - Head Bio   "chicken pellets"   "too much chx in world"
MO — "I don't know nething"
DB - "what are some examples?   what % is chicken

Declining Fish Stocks

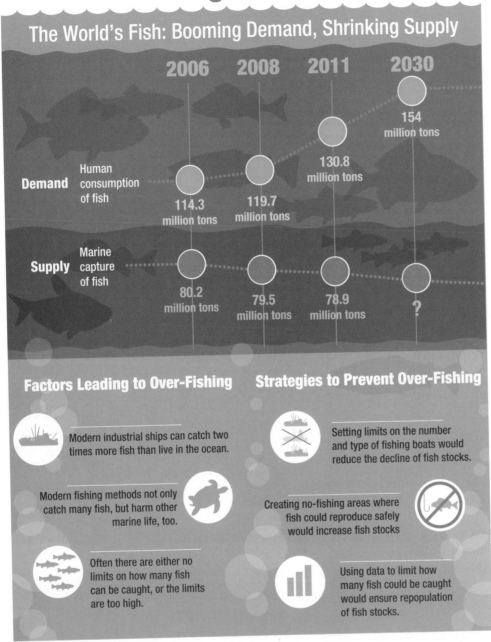

The World's Fish: Booming Demand, Shrinking Supply

		2006	2008	2011	2030

Demand Human consumption of fish

- 114.3 million tons (2006)
- 119.7 million tons (2008)
- 130.8 million tons (2011)
- 154 million tons (2030)

Supply Marine capture of fish

- 80.2 million tons (2006)
- 79.5 million tons (2008)
- 78.9 million tons (2011)
- ? (2030)

Factors Leading to Over-Fishing

Modern industrial ships can catch two times more fish than live in the ocean.

Modern fishing methods not only catch many fish, but harm other marine life, too.

Often there are either no limits on how many fish can be caught, or the limits are too high.

Strategies to Prevent Over-Fishing

Setting limits on the number and type of fishing boats would reduce the decline of fish stocks.

Creating no-fishing areas where fish could reproduce safely would increase fish stocks

Using data to limit how many fish could be caught would ensure repopulation of fish stocks.

Source: Bloomberg Philanthropies

P THINK CRITICALLY Categorize. Work in a small group. Discuss which title matches each description in the bottom section of the infographic. Write the titles in the spaces. Two titles don't match any of the descriptions.

> Destructive Practices   Healthy Options   Ineffective Laws
> Controlled Access   Protected Areas   Smart Limits
> Temporary Solutions   Too Much Capacity

Q COLLABORATE Work with a partner. What things could we do on a personal level to help reduce the problem of over-fishing? Discuss your ideas. Then share them with the class. Which of the ideas do you think Dan Barber would support? Why?

A **THINK CRITICALLY** **Synthesize.** Work with a partner. Discuss these questions. Then share your ideas with another pair of students.

1. Dan Barber's idea worth spreading is about producing sustainable food that is environmentally friendly, healthy, and delicious. Which of these ideas do the professor and students also discuss in Part 1?

2. During the academic discussion, the students discuss three food-production technologies—printing food, aquaponics farms, and growing meat in a laboratory. Which of the three technologies do you think Barber would most support? Why?

B **THINK CRITICALLY** **Reflect.** Answer these questions. Then discuss your responses with a partner.

1. After studying this unit, have your views changed about the importance of sustainable food? Why, or why not?

2. Do you feel technology will have a big impact on the food you eat in the future? Why, or why not?

3. Do you think more farms should focus on relationships, as *Veta la Palma* does? Why, or why not?

COMMUNICATE

ASSIGNMENT: Role-Play an Advertisement Working in a group, you will create an advertisement and a slogan—a short, memorable phrase used to promote a product or service—for one of these types of sustainable foods. Either act out your advertisement or, if you prefer, present your ideas. Review the ideas in Parts 1 and 2 and the listening and speaking skills as you prepare your presentation on one of these foods:

- Vegetables that have been grown aquaponically
- Meat that has been developed in a laboratory
- Fish that has been farmed at *Veta la Palma*

PREPARE

PRESENTATION SKILL Connect with Your Audience

Connecting with your listeners or audience is a great way to deliver a message that will be interesting and memorable. There are several things you can do to connect with your audience effectively. These include:

- Expressing ideas that match the hopes or concerns of your audience
- Talking about topics that are likely to be familiar to your listeners
- Telling stories or giving examples that people understand and can relate to
- Saying things in a humorous or memorable way

(See page 173 in the *Independent Student Handbook* for more information about connecting with your audience.)

C COLLABORATE Work in a small group. Complete the tasks.

1. Decide which type of sustainable food you will create a promotional advertisement for.

2. Come up with an advertisement and a slogan that will connect with your audience.

3. Decide if you will act out your advertisement as a role play or just present your ideas.

4. Decide the role each group member will take when acting out or presenting your advertisement.

5. Rehearse your advertisement or presentation several times until you can deliver it confidently.

D Read the rubric on page 181 before you deliver your advertisement. Notice the evaluation criteria. Keep these categories in mind as you deliver your advertisement and watch those of your classmates.

PRESENT

E Act out or present your advertisement to the rest of the class. Watch the advertisments of the other groups.

F **THINK CRITICALLY** Evaluate. Work in a small group. If possible, each member of your group should have acted out a different advertisement. Share feedback on the advertisements you watched. Say which ads you think would be most likely to make consumers buy the food and why. Say whether you enjoyed acting out the advertisement and why, or why not.

REFLECT

Reflect on what you have learned. Check [✓] your progress.

I can
- ☐ think of questions before, while, and after I listen to improve my understanding.
- ☐ make a note of who says what when I listen to multiple speakers.
- ☐ state what side of an issue I support to help listeners understand my perspective.
- ☐ use connected speech to sound natural when speaking.
- ☐ connect with my listeners or audience in order to deliver a powerful message.

I understand the meanings of these words and can use them.
Circle those you know. Underline those you need to work on.

conception AWL	distribute AWL	filter	nutrient
conventional AWL	drawback	ingredient	purify
conversion AWL	ecological	intensively AWL	realist
deplete	edible	neutral AWL	skeptical
discard	feast	niche	thriving

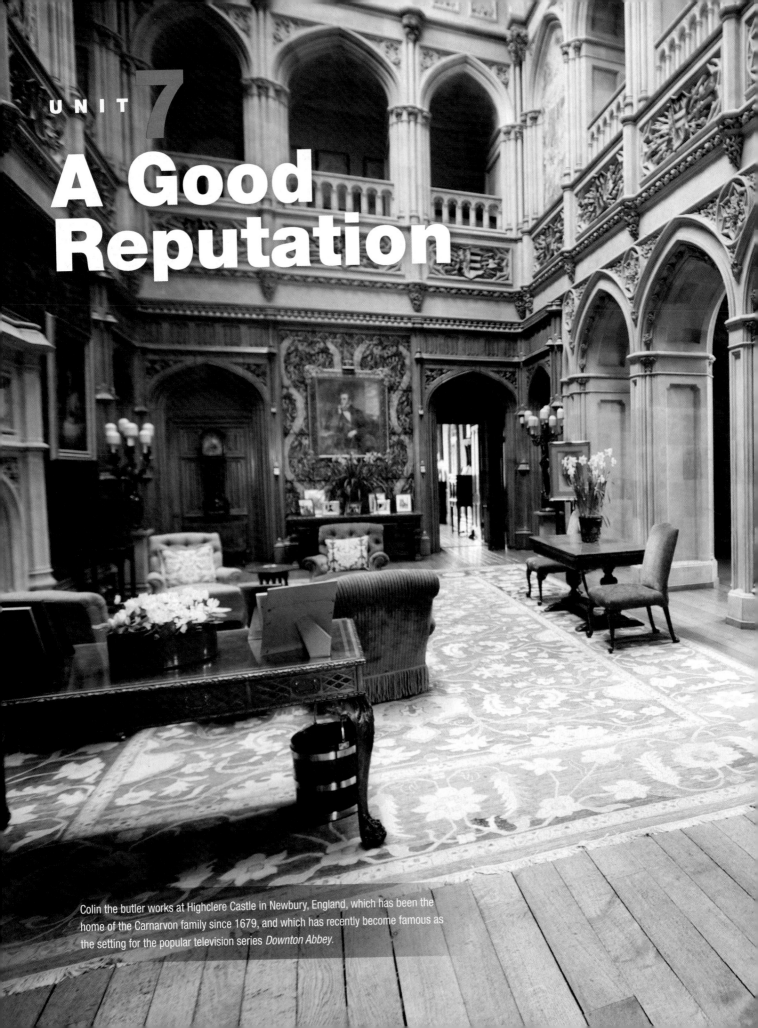

UNIT 7
A Good Reputation

Colin the butler works at Highclere Castle in Newbury, England, which has been the home of the Carnarvon family since 1679, and which has recently become famous as the setting for the popular television series *Downton Abbey*.

THINK AND DISCUSS

1 Look at the photo and read the caption. In order to work as a butler, what characteristics does someone like Colin need? Why? What kind of reputation do families with personal servants typically have? Do you think this reputation is deserved? Support your views.

2 Do you think it is easier to get a good reputation or to lose one? Why?

PART 1 The Art of Reputation

BEFORE YOU LISTEN

A **COMMUNICATE** Work in a small group. Discuss these questions.

1. Do you visit art galleries or art museums? Why, or why not?

2. Which of the two paintings on this page do you like more? Why?

3. Why do you think works by these artists typically sell for millions of dollars?

B **2.19** **COMMUNICATE** Work with a partner. Listen to segment 1 of an academic lecture. Then discuss the questions.

1. Who had a reputation as a great artist both during his life and after his death?

2. Who only got a reputation as a great artist hundreds of years after his death?

3. Can you predict what factors caused the difference in Rembrandt's and Vermeer's reputations?

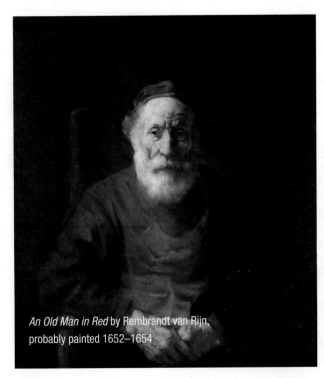

An Old Man in Red by Rembrandt van Rijn, probably painted 1652–1654

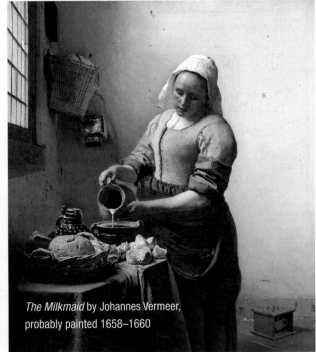

The Milkmaid by Johannes Vermeer, probably painted 1658–1660

124 **UNIT 7** A Good Reputation

VOCABULARY

C 🎧 **2.20** Read and listen to these sentences with words from the lecture. Choose the most likely definition of each bold word.

1. The museum is hosting an exhibition of **portraits** of elderly people by great artists like Rembrandt.
   a. paintings of a head or face   **b.** paintings of famous people   **c.** paintings of adults or children

2. The lives of the artists Vincent van Gogh and Edvard Munch share several interesting **parallels**.
   a. competitions   **b.** similarities   **c.** functions

3. The copy of the painting was so good it was **virtually** impossible to tell it apart from the original.
   a. hardly   **b.** only   **c.** almost

4. The artist received a **commission** to produce a painting celebrating her country's independence.
   a. offer to attend an event   **b.** decision about what to do   **c.** order for a work of art

5. The new Museum of **Contemporary** Art will only display works produced in or after the 1950s.
   a. modern   **b.** expensive   **c.** fashionable

6. In the **assessment** of many art critics, the artist's early work was less powerful than his later pieces.
   a. evaluation   **b.** opportunity   **c.** attraction

7. Among all of the great artists in the world, Leonardo da Vinci perhaps has the highest **standing**.
   a. attitude   **b.** sincerity   **c.** reputation

8. The price of the painting was higher than expected because so many people wanted to **acquire** it.
   a. look at or watch   **b.** buy or obtain   **c.** study or discuss

9. The artist's reputation **waned** after people noticed he was selling works by his students as his own.
   a. declined   **b.** renovated   **c.** lengthened

10. The new exhibition at the National Gallery is sold out because of the many **exceptional** reviews.
    a. surprisingly clear   **b.** generally acceptable   **c.** unusually good

D COMMUNICATE Work with a partner. Take turns answering these questions. Use the words in bold in your answers.

1. What kinds of paintings and photographs do you generally prefer: **portraits** or landscapes? Why?

2. Do you think celebrities, scientists, artists, or teachers should have greater **standing** in society? Why?

3. Do you generally like **contemporary** art, literature, or music? Why?

4. In your **assessment**, who is the best artist, writer, or musician from your country? Why?

5. What is one thing you would love to **acquire?** Why? How much would you be willing to pay for it?

6. What do you think is an example of an **exceptional** piece of art? What makes it so exceptional?

Visitors admire a painting in "The Young Vermeer" exhibition at a museum in Dresden, Germany.

LISTEN

E 🎧 **2.21** ▶ **1.35** **LISTEN FOR MAIN IDEAS** Listen to the lecture. Check (✓) the five factors that the professor says influenced the reputations of Rembrandt and Vermeer.

1. ___✓___ The quality of each artist's paintings

2. ___✓___ Whether or not each artist had students

3. ___✓___ How many people discussed each artist

4. _____ The prices that each artist's work sold for

5. ___✓___ The number of works each artist produced

6. ___✓___ Each artist's links with people of high status

F 🎧 **2.22** **LISTEN FOR DETAILS** Listen to segment 2 of the lecture. Write T if a statement is *true* or F if it is *false*. Then work with a partner to correct the false statements.

1. ___F___ Rembrandt was born in Leiden in 1606 and moved to Amsterdam in 16~~21~~. [3]

2. ___T___ During his life, Rembrandt gained a good reputation for painting portraits.

3. ___T___ Rembrandt created thousands of drawings and hundreds of paintings and prints.

4. ___T___ Vermeer was born in Delft in 1632 and died without much money in 1675.

5. ___F___ Vermeer joined a Delft association of painters while he was in his ~~late~~ *early* 20s.

6. ___F___ There is evidence to suggest that Vermeer created up to 4̶0̶ *3–4* paintings a year.

LISTENING SKILL **Identify the Speaker's Purpose**

Understanding the purpose, or reason, why a speaker says something can help you follow his or her ideas more easily. Sometimes, speakers will introduce their purposes explicitly, either with specific phrases or with rhetorical questions:

I mention this because . . .	*Why have I mentioned this?*
This is important because . . .	*Why is this important?*
This matters because . . .	*Why does this matter?*

Often, however, you will have to infer the speaker's reason for saying something. In the example below, we can infer that the speaker's purpose is to emphasize the reputation of the two artists although he does not state this explicitly.

The paintings of Rembrandt and Vermeer sell for millions of dollars at auction, and they are considered among the greatest artists in history.

G ⌒ **2.23** **IDENTIFY SPEAKER'S PURPOSE** Listen to segment 3, which includes excerpts from the lecture. Choose the statement that best describes the speaker's purpose.

1. The speaker talks about why Rembrandt's reputation immediately after his death survived better than Vermeer's. His purpose is

   Why? (written in margin)

   a. to introduce several factors that explain this.

   b. to define what *reputation* means.

2. He talks about how many works each artist produced. His purpose is

   a. to state how it's better to have quantity rather than quality.

   b. to give a reason why art lovers discussed Rembrandt more than Vermeer.

3. He says that Rembrandt tutored many students. His purpose is

   a. to explain why Rembrandt's name spread more widely during his lifetime than Vermeer's name during his.

   b. to show that Rembrandt was a better teacher than Vermeer.

4. He mentioned where the two artists lived and worked. His purpose is

   This is imp. b/c (written in margin)

   a. to show that Delft was not the center of the art world.

   b. to emphasize that influential people knew Rembrandt's work.

5. He describes the social position of the two artists. His purpose is

   a. to argue that it was easier to make money as an artist if you were from the upper classes.

   b. to argue that people of higher social standing were more likely to be discussed and remembered.

H ⌒ **2.23** **COMMUNICATE** Work with a partner. Discuss the questions. Listen to the excerpts again if necessary.

1. In which excerpts does the speaker state his purpose directly? What phrases or questions does he use?

2. Did you find it more difficult to recognize his purpose in some excerpts than in others? Why do you think this was?

AFTER YOU LISTEN

I **THINK CRITICALLY** Evaluate. Check (✓) the main reason why you think Vermeer didn't have a reputation as a great artist immediately after his death. Then share your idea and your reasons with a partner.

_____ He didn't have connections to members of the Dutch social elite.

_____ He didn't have any students who could produce similar works.

_____ He produced only a small number of paintings.

_____ He spent his whole life in a city that was not a center of art.

VERMEER BY THE NUMBERS

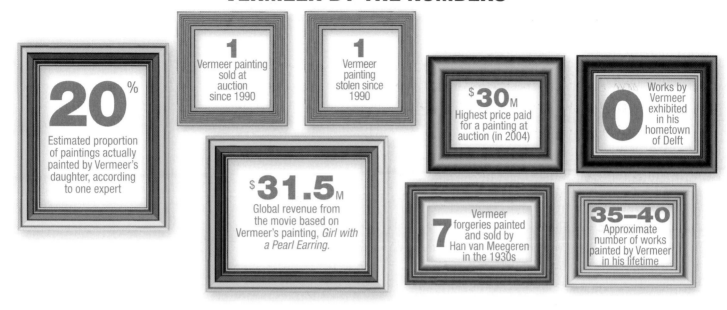

20% Estimated proportion of paintings actually painted by Vermeer's daughter, according to one expert

1 Vermeer painting sold at auction since 1990

1 Vermeer painting stolen since 1990

$30M Highest price paid for a painting at auction (in 2004)

0 Works by Vermeer exhibited in his hometown of Delft

$31.5M Global revenue from the movie based on Vermeer's painting, *Girl with a Pearl Earring*.

7 Vermeer forgeries painted and sold by Han van Meegeren in the 1930s

35–40 Approximate number of works painted by Vermeer in his lifetime

J COMMUNICATE Work in a small group. Look at the data about Vermeer. Then discuss these questions.

1. Which of the details, if any, did you already know?

2. Which of the details are most surprising to you? Why?

3. Which of the details would you like to know more about? What would you like to know?

SPEAKING

SPEAKING SKILL Help Listeners Follow Your Ideas

Good speakers understand that it can be difficult for listeners to follow their ideas and arguments. To help listeners follow their ideas, they can:

1. **Repeat** or emphasize key ideas and arguments.

2. **Define** or give an example of unclear or unfamiliar things.

3. **Answer** unspoken questions listeners might have (sometimes by asking a rhetorical question).

4. **Explain** why information is important.

(See pages 164–165 in the *Independent Student Handbook* for more information about speaking so that listeners can follow.)

The painting *Young Woman Seated at the Virginal* by Vermeer sold for $30 million at auction in London in 2004.

K 🎧 **2.24** Listen to segment 4, which includes four excerpts from the lecture. What is the main way the professor helps students follow his ideas in each excerpt? Write *Repeat*, *Define*, *Answer*, or *Explain*.

1. _A_____ why?_____
2. _~~REPR~~ E_____
3. _E / A_____
4. _D / E_____

L **COMMUNICATE** Work in a small group. Can you think of other artists, authors, actors, or musicians whose reputations have increased or declined after they died? Why do you think this happened? Discuss your ideas with your group. As you speak, help your listeners follow your ideas.

PRONUNCIATION SKILL **Use Emphasis for a Purpose**

To emphasize a word, you may make the vowel in the stressed syllable longer, say the word more loudly, and/or raise or lower the pitch (tone) on the word. Speakers emphasize words and phrases for many reasons. These include:

🎧 **2.25**

- To correct a mistake or misunderstanding

    This happened in **1631**, **not** *1630.*

- To highlight how one idea differs from another

    Rembrandt lived in **Amsterdam**, *while Vermeer lived in* **Delft**.

- To make a key detail or major point clear

    What's the reason? One word: **reputation**.

M 🎧 **2.26** **COMMUNICATE** Work with a partner. Discuss the word(s) in each excerpt from the lecture that you think the speaker emphasizes, and why. Then listen to segment 5 and underline the word(s) that the speaker emphasizes.

1. *"They are considered among the greatest artists in history. But for one of them, this was not always true."*

2. *"It's hard to give an exact figure, but evidence suggests that he might have painted just 40 works in his entire career."*

3. *"But the contemporary assessment is that both Rembrandt and Vermeer are true Dutch Masters. So why did Vermeer's standing improve? One word: quality."*

4. *"An artist's name may be forgotten, but if he or she creates art of exceptional quality then, eventually, his or her reputation will grow."*

N Work with a different partner. What other words could the professor have emphasized in the excerpts in exercise M? Read each excerpt aloud and emphasize these words. How does the meaning of the excerpt change?

The currency of the new economy is trust

" Reputation will be the currency that says that you can trust me. "

BEFORE YOU WATCH

A THINK CRITICALLY Predict. Work in a small group. Read the title of the TED Talk, the information about the speaker, and the two definitions below. Then discuss what you think this talk will be about.

currency (n) – something, usually money, that is used to pay for goods, services, or something of value

new economy (n) – new technological industries, such as the Internet, that often have high growth

RACHEL BOTSMAN Sharing Innovator

Rachel Botsman is an expert on the power of sharing in the "new economy"—the fast-growing world of online service-based industries. She originated the concept of "collaborative consumption"—the idea that groups of people can share the use and the cost of a good or service. Botsman believes this concept will change many aspects of society including the way we work, shop, and live.

B COMMUNICATE Work with a partner. Discuss the questions.

1. Botsman begins her talk in this way: "So if someone asked you for the three words that would sum up your reputation, what would you say?" How would you answer her question?

2. In what ways is your reputation important? What can you do to protect it? To strengthen it?

3. In what ways do you think trust and reputation are currencies in the new economy?

VOCABULARY

C 🔊 **2.27** These definitions will help you learn words in the TED Talk. Read and listen to the sentences. Then write the letter of the best definition from page 133 for each bold word in the space.

1. _____ The company's biggest **asset** was its positive reputation among consumers.

2. _____ They reduced energy **consumption** to attract environmentally conscious customers.

3. _____ This new service **empowers** people by giving them access to useful online resources.

4. _____ The **core** of her plan was excellent, but many of the details were not fully developed.

5. _____ He could not complete the **transaction** because the Web site would not accept his credit card.

6. _____ The firm saved a lot of money when it chose to **outsource** training and recruitment to another company.

7. _____ Her **bid** for the project won because she had earned a great reputation from previous work.

8. _____ The employee promised to return and finish the work after he had run a quick **errand**.

9. _____ She was so happy with the product that she gave it a five-star **rating** in an online review.

10. _____ Smartphones created a **revolution** in how people communicate with others.

a. (n) a big change caused by technology or events

b. (n) a short journey to do a task or get something

c. (n) a valuable skill, person, quality, or advantage

d. (n) an offer to do some work for a certain price

e. (n) an opinion about the quality of something

f. (n) the act of doing business or buying something

g. (n) the act of using, eating, or buying something

h. (n) the central or most important part of something

i. (v) give somebody confidence, power, or authority

j. (v) use an external company to provide something

D COMMUNICATE Work with a partner. Take turns responding to these questions. Use the words in bold in your answers.

1. In your opinion, what **assets** do people need to succeed in life these days?

2. Think about a time when you felt **empowered**. What gave you this feeling?

3. In general, do you think it is good for firms to **outsource** services? Why, or why not?

4. What is an interesting **errand** you ran for someone else? Why was it interesting?

5. What is one product you have used that you would give a five-star **rating** to? Why?

6. What online services, if any, have caused a social **revolution?** Support your view.

WATCH

learn**more** The online collaborative economy is a billion-dollar industry with five main markets:

- Goods—e.g., Etsy: an online marketplace where designers and other creative people sell their works

- Money—e.g., Kickstarter: a "crowdfunding" site where people look for funding to develop a project

- Transportation—e.g., Uber: a service that allows people to use an app to find a driver to take them somewhere

- Space—e.g., Airbnb: an online site that helps people find places to stay in other people's homes

- Services—e.g., TaskRabbit: a site that lets consumers outsource certain tasks to other people

E ▷ **1.36** **WATCH FOR MAIN IDEAS** Work in a small group. Read the idea worth spreading and discuss what it means. Then watch the edited TED Talk in four segments and complete the tasks below.

> Rachel Botsman's idea worth spreading is that technology is creating marketplaces that are based on trust and personal reputation.

1. What is the main idea of each segment? Write the correct segment number (1–4) for each statement. Two statements are not main ideas.

   a. __2__ A key aspect of collaborative consumption is helping people connect with and trust others.

   b. _____ Online marketplaces like Airbnb help people develop close relationships with strangers.

   c. __3__ People who are efficient and who can be trusted are likely to do well in the new economy.

   d. __1__ Because of the age we live in, reputation is a key asset that people need to protect.

   e. _____ The collaborative economy makes it easier for people who have lost their jobs to find work.

   f. __4__ Reputation leads to trust, which leads to value in the real world and this will have a big impact on society.

2. Is the main idea of each segment directly or indirectly related to Botsman's idea worth spreading? Discuss and support your views.

   A: *For me, the main idea in segment 2 is directly related to the idea worth spreading because both statements mention trust.*

   B: *True, but the idea worth spreading doesn't focus on collaboration, so isn't it indirect?*

NOTE-TAKING SKILL **Note Numbers and Their Relevance**

Speakers often support their ideas with numbers such as amounts, dates, prices, or percentages. It is usually helpful to make a note of numbers that you hear. It is also important to note other information about the number, especially how it is related to the speaker's points. Look at a short example of some notes about the TED Talk:

"Let's just take a look at Chris. You can see that over 200 people have given him an average rating over 4.99 out of 5."

Chris = 200 ppl gave him 4.99/5 avg rating

WORDS IN THE TALK

enrich (v): to make richer or to improve
micro-entrepreneur (n): someone who operates a very small business
peer-to-peer marketplace (n): an online economic system whereby people can buy and sell products or services directly from each other
rigorous (adj): difficult or having high standards
secret sauce (n): the main (and sometimes secret) reason why something is successful

F ▶ **1.37** **WATCH FOR DETAILS** Watch segment 3 of the edited TED Talk again and take notes. Focus on the numbers you hear. Then use your notes to match each number to the relevant detail (a–f).

1. 4 _f_

2. 20 _e_

3. 70 _c_

4. over 100 _d_

5. 4,000 _a_

6. 5,000 _b_

a. people in the U.S. who currently work as Rabbits

b. people in the U.S. who are waiting to start working as Rabbits

c. percentage of workers who were unemployed or underemployed before

d. times each day the most common task is posted on TaskRabbit

e. years it took people to learn to fully trust others online

f. years since Chris Mok lost his job as an art buyer

G Work with a partner. Use the notes you took in exercise F to complete the notes below with either a number or a short explanation of a number's relevance.

1. *forty-six* = _Chris' age_

2. *stages in TR interview process* = _4_

3. *num laundry loads done by TR* = _12.5_

4. *$ Mok earns/mth* = _5000_

H **THINK CRITICALLY** **Infer.** Work with a partner. Read these excerpts from Botsman's talk. What is her purpose in making each statement? Write *a*, *b*, or *c*. Check your answers with a partner.

a. To illustrate something that did not have a market before but does now

b. To highlight the importance of building and maintaining one's online reputation

c. To show how collaborative marketplaces can build trust between strangers

1. _a_ *"If you don't like the hotel, there's a castle down the road that you can rent for $5,000 a night."*

2. _c_ *"It's about empowering people to make meaningful connections . . . by engaging in marketplaces."*

3. _b_ *"She would refrain from leaving a bad review on one condition: He got a cat. And so Sebastian bought Squeak to protect his reputation."*

4. _a_ *"The number-one task posted, over 100 times a day, is something that many of us have felt the pain of doing: yes, assembling Ikea furniture."*

5. _b_ *"What Chris has noted is that as his reputation has gone up, so has his chance of winning a bid and how much he can charge."*

Airbnb guests could win a chance to sleep surrounded by sharks at the aquarium in Paris, France.

I ▶ **1.38 IDENTIFY THE SPEAKER'S PURPOSE** Work with a partner. Watch segment 5, which includes two excerpts from the edited TED Talk. Then discuss the questions.

1. What is Botsman's purpose in telling the story about Sebastian's former guests contacting him? *To illustrate how its about meaningful conn. explicit*

2. What is her purpose in mentioning how much money Chris Mok makes each month? *To show how much impact it has on someones life – implicit now its like currency*

3. In the excerpts, does Botsman state her purpose explicitly, or does she imply it? How do you know?

J ▶ **1.39 FOLLOW IDEAS** Watch segment 6, which includes three excerpts from the edited TED Talk. How does Botsman help the audience follow her ideas? Write *a*, *b*, or *c*. Check your answers with a partner.

a. She repeats or emphasizes a key idea or argument.

b. She defines or gives an example of something unclear or unfamiliar.

c. She answers unspoken questions that people might have.

1. _C_ *"How would people describe your judgment, your knowledge, your behaviors, in different situations? Today I'd like to explore with you why the answer to this question will become profoundly important."*

2. _B_ *"Now, as many of you know, Airbnb is a peer-to-peer marketplace that matches people who have space to rent with people who are looking for a place to stay in over 192 countries."*

3. _a_ *"Because at its core, it's about empowerment. It's about empowering people to make meaningful connections, connections that are enabling us to rediscover a humanness that we've lost somewhere along the way."*

K ▶ **1.40** **EXPAND YOUR VOCABULARY** Watch the excerpts from the TED Talk. Guess the meanings of the phrases in the box.

> catch up with someone   refrain from   hit home
> weed out   labor force

L **WATCH MORE** Go to TED.com to watch the full TED Talk by Rachel Botsman.

AFTER YOU WATCH

M **THINK CRITICALLY** **Interpret an Infographic.** Work with a partner. Look at the infographic. Then discuss the questions. When you have finished, share your ideas with another pair of students.

1. Which of the four core categories does each of the sample tasks belong to? If a task does not match any of the core categories, discuss what category it could belong to.

2. Think of some other examples of tasks that match the four core categories.

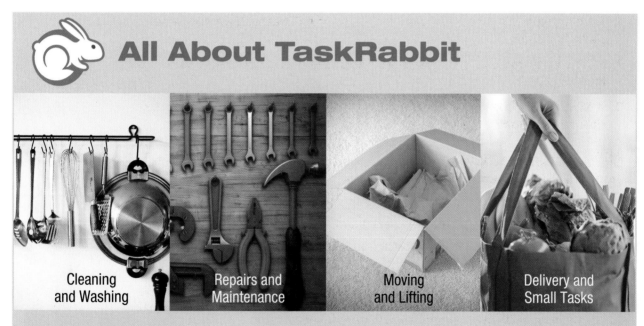

All About TaskRabbit

Cleaning and Washing   Repairs and Maintenance   Moving and Lifting   Delivery and Small Tasks

Number of Tasks
- Mounting 16,000 TVs on walls
- Spending 350,000 hours running errands
- Washing and folding 12,500 loads of laundry
- Carrying furniture up and down 4,000,000 stairs
- Assembling the equivalent of 52,000 Ikea bookcases

Unusual Tasks
- Retrieving a set of keys from the bottom of a lake
- Writing a letter to win back an ex-girlfriend
- Bringing kittens to an office so workers could play with them
- Covering somebody's entire desk, including the computer, in plastic wrap

Sources: Botsman's TED Talk; TaskRabbit, Inc.; BostInno; Urbanful

N **THINK CRITICALLY** Personalize. Work in a small group. Discuss these questions.

1. Would you be willing to pay somebody to do each of the tasks listed in the "Number of Tasks" section of the infographic? Why, or why not?

2. Which of the unusual tasks would you be willing to do? Why? How much would you charge? What strange task would you ask somebody else to do?

O **COMMUNICATE** Work in a small group. Discuss these questions.

1. Botsman says that technology is making it easier *"to build trust between strangers."* To what extent do you think she is correct?

2. Botsman says that *"new trust networks, and the reputation capital they generate, will reinvent the way we think about wealth, markets, power, and personal identity."* How might trust and reputation impact the wealth, power, and identity of a business or a person?

P **COMMUNICATE** Work with a partner to discuss these questions. Use the techniques from the speaking skill box on page 129 to help listeners follow your ideas.

1. Would you rather be an Airbnb guest and stay in somebody else's home or be an Airbnb host and have other people staying in your home? Why?

2. Can you think of a time when you did something in order to gain a good reputation or avoid getting a bad reputation? What happened?

3. Will you change either your behavior or the online sites you visit after watching Botsman's talk? Why and how, or why not?

Livi planters can stick onto anything—glass, walls, or your refrigerator—so even if you don't have a lot of space or natural sunshine, you can grow plants inside. Designer Hooman Koliji launched *Livi* on Kickstarter, a collaborative consumption marketplace.

Put It Together

A THINK CRITICALLY Synthesize. Work in a small group. Complete these tasks.

1. Read the four ideas below and indicate where they are from.

   Ideas in academic lecture: _____ _____

   Ideas in Botsman's talk: _____ _____

   a. A person's reputation usually rises if influential people talk about the person or his or her work.

   b. Reputation is a way to measure how much other people in a community trust somebody.

   c. The most valuable asset a person has is his or her reputation because reputation builds trust.

   d. A person's reputation will eventually rise if he or she does work of exceptional quality.

2. Look at the two ideas expressed in the academic lecture. Do you think Botsman would agree that these ideas also influence reputation these days? Why, or why not?

3. Look at the two ideas expressed by Botsman. Do you think her ideas would have been true in the time of Rembrandt and Vermeer, too? Why, or why not?

B COMMUNICATE Botsman says that our online reputation will be our "most valuable asset" in the future. What do you do to build and protect yours? Discuss with a partner.

COMMUNICATE

ASSIGNMENT: Present a Case Study You are going to work individually to present a case study describing a Web site or Web service that you know well and for which the reputation of users is important in some way. Review the ideas in Parts 1 and 2 and the listening and speaking skills as you prepare your case study.

PREPARE

C Choose one of the following sites below for your case study. Choose a site that you are familiar with. It should also be one for which the reputation of users is important in some way.

- A collaborative consumption marketplace such as Airbnb, Etsy, Uber, Kickstarter, or TaskRabbit

- A social networking site such as Facebook or LinkedIn

- A Web site where product or service reviews are featured such as Amazon or Yelp

- Your own idea: _____

D Make notes about what you will say when you present your case study. Organize your presentation in the following way:

1. Describe the Web site—What product/service does it offer?

2. Describe the profile of the typical users of the site—Why do they use it? How does the site meet their needs better than others?

3. Describe how reputation of users is important—How can users gain or lose reputation?

4. Describe your own experiences using the site.

5. Describe how using the site has affected your life—Has it improved your reputation? Have you improved the reputation of others?

6. Conclude by saying whether you would recommend using this site to others.

E COLLABORATE Work with a partner. Take turns rehearsing your case studies. After each turn, give each other feedback about how to improve the presentation, especially in terms of using effective supporting details, helping listeners follow your ideas, and making your purpose clear.

F Read the rubric on page 182 before you present. Notice how your case study will be evaluated. Keep these categories in mind as you deliver your presentation and watch your classmates' presentations.

PRESENT

G Give your presentation to the class. Watch your classmates' presentations. Make a note of any numbers the speakers use, and their relevance. Try to understand each speaker's purpose when he or she makes a particular point.

H THINK CRITICALLY Evaluate. Work in a small group. Share feedback on the case studies you watched and listen to feedback about your case study. As you exchange feedback, complete these tasks.

1. Tell the people in your group what you were pleased with about your presentation, and why.

2. Say what you will do better next time, and why.

3. Say if you are interested in trying out any of the sites you learned about, and why, or why not.

REFLECT

Reflect on what you have learned. Check [✓] your progress.

I can
- [ ] identify the speaker's purpose when listening.
- [ ] help listeners follow ideas and arguments when speaking.
- [ ] have a clear purpose when emphasizing words.
- [ ] take note of numbers and their relevance to the speaker's points.
- [ ] include effective supporting details when giving a presentation.

I understand the meanings of these words and can use them.
Circle those you know. Underline those you need to work on.

acquire AWL	consumption AWL	exceptional	revolution AWL
assessment AWL	contemporary AWL	outsource	standing
asset	core AWL	parallel AWL	transaction
bid	empower	portrait	virtually AWL
commission AWL	errand	rating	wane

Life Hacks

8.4 HOURS
Video recorded

369 MINS
Sleep per night

582
Photos taken

11,726
Steps walked

A man wears several tracking devices to monitor various aspects of his body, his behavior, and his life.

143 BPM
Maximum heart rate

3,324
Activity score

3,089
Calories burned

THINK AND DISCUSS

1 Look at the photo and read the caption. The man is wearing seven different devices. What do you think each of them measures? Would you ever wear similar devices? Why, or why not?

2 "Life hacks" are ways of doing something that can help you live your life better or more efficiently. What aspects of your life would you like to improve? Why?

BEFORE YOU LISTEN

A **COMMUNICATE** Work in a small group. Discuss these questions.

1. Look at the photo and read the caption. What do you think *self-tracking* means?

2. Do you ever track information about your life? If yes, what do you track, how, and why? If no, why not?

B **COMMUNICATE** Work in a small group. You are going to hear a conversation between two students, one of whom has recently improved his health, finances, and grades. Which of these improvements would you most like in your life? Why? How would you go about improving this area of your life? Discuss.

Suran Goonatilake steps into a 3D body scanner once a month to map his body shape and record his measurements. "One of the best predictors of heart disease is the size of your belly," he says. The body scanner lets him know if he should modify his exercise routine or diet.

VOCABULARY

C 🎧 **2.28** Read and listen to the sentences with words from the conversation. Then complete each definition with the correct form of one of the bold words.

a. Professor Yee's ability to remember the names of all the students in her classes is **impressive**.

b. Kay got a personal tracking device to record and **quantify** data about her physical activity.

c. Professor Evans had students **interpret** the data from their experiments for homework.

d. When he first began attending college, Gavin **suffered** from homesickness for a few weeks.

e. During her time at college, Chandra **accumulated** dozens of textbooks and study guides.

f. Alex did the experiment so carefully he was able to get more **precise** results than anyone else.

g. Although she spent hours commuting, it never **occurred to** Anne to move closer to campus.

h. Most students' favorite **aspect** of Professor Chen's class was his habit of telling funny stories.

i. After Jake worked hard to raise his GPA to 3.5, he became **eligible** to apply for the scholarship.

j. Leon was **tempted** to apply for a part-time job, but decided it was better to focus on his studies.

1. _precise_ (adj) being very exact or accurate

2. _impressive_ (adj) having some very positive qualities that people admire

3. _eligible_ (adj) having the right to do or be chosen for something

4. _aspect_ (n) a part or feature of something, such as a situation or subject

5. _accumulated_ (v) add up, collect, and increase over time

6. _suffered_ (v) experience something negative, such as pain or loss

7. _occurred to_ (v) have an idea or thought about something

8. _tempted_ (v) have a strong desire or interest in doing something

9. _quantify_ (v) measure and state the amount of something

10. _interpret_ (v) understand something and explain its meaning

D COMMUNICATE Complete the sentences in your own words. Then take turns sharing your sentences with another student and asking why he or she holds each view.

1. The most **impressive** person I have ever met is _____.

2. In my life, I have **accumulated** dozens of _____.

3. It is important to be **precise** when you are _____.

4. One enjoyable **aspect** of learning English is _____.

5. When people turn 18, they should be **eligible** to _____.

6. If I had enough money, I would be **tempted** to _____.

LISTEN

E 🎧 **2.29 LISTEN FOR MAIN IDEAS** Work with a partner. Listen to the conversation between Abdel and Reg. Read Abdel's email summary of the conversation. Complete his email with phrases from the box. Two phrases won't be used.

> attending a meeting   discussing what to do   resigning from his job
> improving as a person   interpreting the data   tracking information

I bumped into my friend Reg earlier. He's really changed his life since I last saw him. He's doing this thing called "the quantified self." It involves _tracking info_ about many aspects of your life and using that data to improve your situation. He tracked his expenses for a while and after _interpreting the data_, he saw that by selling his car, _resigning from his job_, and moving closer to campus, he would reduce his expenses. Since then, his health, grades, and finances have all improved. I found his story so impressive that I'm _attending a meeting_ with him later this week to learn more about the quantified self.

F ⌢ 2.30 **LISTEN FOR DETAILS** Read some of the changes to Reg's life that resulted from self-tracking. Then listen to segment 2 of the conversation and number the changes in the order that Reg mentions them.

___2___ **a.** cooking his own meals   ___5___ **d.** improving his grades

___4___ **b.** cutting his medical bills   ___3___ **e.** losing some weight

___6___ **c.** getting a scholarship   ___1___ **f.** walking and exercising more

---

LISTENING SKILL Recognize a Speaker's Attitude

Recognizing a speaker's attitude about something can help you understand his or her feelings even if they are not stated directly. There are three things to focus on when interpreting a speaker's attitude:

1. Tone

A high or rising tone often indicates a strong positive feeling, such as excitement, or a strong negative feeling, such as irritation. A lower or falling tone, on the other hand, may indicate a negative attitude.

2. Speech rate

A fast speech rate may indicate that a speaker has a strong feeling—either positive or negative—about something. In contrast, a slower speech rate may indicate the speaker has a calm or neutral attitude.

3. Language

A speaker's choice of words is a good indicator of attitude. Generally, positive expressions indicate a positive view, and negative or critical phrases suggest a negative one. Notice the difference in these sentences:

Self-tracking takes discipline, but can offer really useful information that's easy to implement.

Self-tracking takes far too much time and gives useless information that's impractical to act on.

G ⌢ 2.31 Listen to segment 3, which includes five excerpts from the conversation. Write the excerpt number next to the attitude you hear. One word won't be used.

confused   ___1___   irritated   ___3___

excited   ___5___   pessimistic   _____

impressed   ___4___   surprised   ___2___

H **COMMUNICATE** Work with a partner. Compare your answers in exercise G. Then discuss what clues helped you recognize the speaker's attitude in each case.

AFTER YOU LISTEN

I **COMMUNICATE** Work in a small group. Discuss the questions.

   1. In the conversation, Reg talks about his fitness tracker. Do you know what a fitness tracker is? Have you ever used one? Share what you know.

   2. What are some advantages of using a fitness tracker? Are there any disadvantages?

J **COMMUNICATE** Imagine you could design your own fitness tracker. From the options below, choose the four features you would find most useful. Then interview three other students to learn what four features they would choose. Make a note of their names and responses.

 1. Thermometer to measure your body temperature

 5. GPS (global positioning satellite) to measure your location

 2. Sensor to measure your heart rate

 6. Environmental sensor to measure air quality and temperature

 3. Sensor to measure the quality of your sleep

 7. Watch, stopwatch, and timer to measure how long an activity takes

 4. Pedometer to count how many steps you have taken

 8. Bright LED flashlight to use at night

K **COLLABORATE** Report the results of your interviews to the class. Tell the name of each interviewee and say which features he or she chose. Your teacher will keep track of the results. Which features were most popular among men? Among women?

SPEAKING

Express Your View Strongly

Sometimes you may wish to let listeners know that you hold a very strong opinion or are completely certain about something. There are several ways you can express a strong point of view. These include:

1. Using modals 🖎

These auxiliary verbs express the strength of your statement.

You can do that . . . (normal)   *You must do that . . .* (strong)

2. Using adverbs of degree

Adverbs such as *really*, *truly*, or *extremely* emphasize the strength of your views by modifying either a verb or an adjective.

I believe that . . . (normal)   *I truly believe that . . .* (strong)

I'm disappointed that . . . (normal)   *I'm extremely disappointed that . . .* (strong)

3. Using the subjunctive after certain adjectives 🖎

The subjunctive is a grammatical pattern that emphasizes something important or urgent. Subjunctive sentences use the base form of verbs (without *to*). Some adjectives that take the subjunctive include *essential*, *important*, and *imperative*. The subjunctive is rare in informal speech.

Maybe he should go . . . (normal)   *It is essential that he go . . .* (strong)

L **COLLABORATE** Work with a partner. Underline the words or phrases in these excerpts from the conversation that indicate the speaker is expressing a strong opinion.

1. *"So you've lost weight and sorted out your finances? That's really impressive. What's your secret?"*

2. *"I have a fitness tracker, and I truly think it's great. It really helps me stay active and keep in shape."*

3. *"I was absolutely certain that my only option was to take a semester or two off and work full-time."*

4. *"I doubted it would help, to be honest, but it was essential that I do something, so I gave it a try."*

5. *"You should totally do it. It'll change your life."*

M COMMUNICATE Decide which three of the statements below you agree with most strongly. Then work with a partner. Take turns explaining why you agree strongly with the statements you each chose.

> A: *I agree strongly that doctors really must be open and transparent with their patients because patients who are sick are often scared, and if their doctor isn't open, they could be more scared.*
>
> B: *That's a good point. For me, I definitely think that smiling can help people live longer, healthier lives. We learned about this in Unit 1, and the evidence that the speaker gave was convincing.*

1. Smiling can help people live longer, healthier lives.
2. Doctors should be open and transparent with their patients.
3. In order to help people, we should listen to them.
4. Big data has the power to solve the world's problems.
5. Understanding our fears can help us prepare for the future.
6. Farmers can produce food that's good for us and the planet.
7. Reputation is becoming a more and more important asset.
8. Analyzing data can help us get better at things.

PRONUNCIATION SKILL **Stress and Intonation in Comparisons and Contrasts**

When you are comparing or contrasting, use stress and intonation to clarify your points.

🎧 **2.32**

1. Stress—Stress the words that show comparison or contrast, or the things or ideas that are being compared.

*This new fitness tracker cost **less** than my old one, but it has **more features**.*

*The **data** I got from self-tracking was more useful than the **advice** from my sister.*

*Although this fitness tracker is **cheap**, its features are **impressive**.*

2. Intonation—In sentences that contrast a positive idea with a negative one, use rising intonation on the positive and falling on the negative.

Tracking your life is great, but it can take a lot of time.

N 🎧 **2.33 COLLABORATE** Work with a partner. Underline the words in these excerpts that should be stressed, and add an arrow to the words that should have a rising or falling intonation. Then listen to the excerpts to check your answers.

1. "As you know, I had money troubles last semester. I got a part-time job, but it wasn't enough. I needed to earn more. And because I was working, I had less time to study."

2. "It occurred to me that if I used those extra dollars to get a better apartment that was closer to campus, I wouldn't need a car at all."

3. "I've got more time to study than before. My grades are so much better that I'm eligible for a scholarship this semester."

O **COLLABORATE** Write a response to each question. Discuss your responses with a partner. Then share your responses with the class using natural stress and intonation.

1. Which is more likely to improve your life—cooking for yourself or walking every day? Why?

   _____

2. Which would be easier for you to do—improve your grades or reduce your expenses? Why?

   _____

3. Which would be the better way to buy a fitness tracker—online or in person? Why?

   _____

4. Whose advice would you trust more—a famous person's or a friend's? Why?

   _____

5. How do you learn best—by watching or by doing? Give examples.

   _____

6. Which skill do you practice more than the others—listening, reading, speaking, or writing? Why?

   _____

PART 2

TEDTALKS

Lies, damned lies, and statistics (about TED Talks)

❝ Could you reverse engineer a TED Talk? Could you create the ultimate TED Talk? **❞**

BEFORE YOU WATCH

A **COMMUNICATE** Work in a small group. Read the short text below and the information about the speaker. Then discuss the questions.

The title of Sebastian Wernicke's TED Talk is part of a famous quote about dishonesty: "There are three kinds of false statements: lies, damned lies, and statistics." This quote implies that statistics are the worst kind of false statement because they can be used to support any argument or opinion, even a weak one.

1. In your view, is Wernicke likely to agree that statistics are the worst kind of lie? Why, or why not?

2. Do you think Wernicke uses this quote as his title to be serious, humorous, or both? Why?

SEBASTIAN WERNICKE Data Scientist

Sebastian Wernicke studied bioinformatics, the science of collecting and analyzing complex biological data. He also trained as a statistician, an expert in collecting and analyzing numbers. He currently works as the head data scientist at Solon, a company based in Germany that offers consulting services to the media, entertainment, telecommunications, and technology industries.

B **THINK CRITICALLY** Identify and Infer. Read the quote on Wernicke's photo. To reverse engineer something means to analyze it in detail in order to find out how it is made and then either copy it or improve it. Discuss these questions in a different small group.

1. Which of these are examples of reverse engineering?
   a. A company that develops a cheap smartphone app after using and analyzing a similar but more expensive app developed by another company
   b. An online bookstore that notices which books are currently popular among customers and offers those books at a discounted price
   c. A person who regularly eats a favorite dish at a restaurant and teaches himself how to make a dish at home that tastes and looks the same

2. What process do you think people use when they reverse engineer something?

3. In your view, what could Wernicke learn from reverse engineering a TED Talk?

© marketoonist.com

VOCABULARY

C 🎧 **2.34** These sentences will help you learn words in the TED Talk. Read and listen to the sentences. Then choose one word from each sentence to complete the definitions.

1. The speaker gave some examples of things she had learned from **statistical** analysis of the data.

   statistical (adj) – relating to the use of statistics, which are a collection of numbers or

   _____

2. Because the speaker's online talk had the best ratings, it was chosen as the **ultimate** presentation.

   ultimate (adj) – being the _____ or most extreme example of something

3. The two effects did not seem linked, but studies proved they were actually strongly **correlated**.

   correlate (v) – show one thing is dependent on or _____ to another thing

4. There is no **concrete** proof yet, but further research should allow us to prove the theory for certain.

   concrete (adj) – relating to something that is real, specific, or _____

5. Students were advised to discuss broad themes in their talks, but to avoid **generalizing** too much.

   generalize (v) – make a _____, general statement about something

6. The woman's talk **featured** some incredible photographs of her exciting new discovery.

   feature (v) – include or have something, such as in a _____ or text, because it is important

7. Because he was worried that audience members without a scientific background would find his talk too **technical**, the speaker worked hard to simplify it.

   technical (adj) – relating to a specific skill or something _____

8. The professor ended her class with some important announcements, including how **imperative** it was that students submit their final papers by the due date.

   imperative (adj) – being especially necessary, _____, or urgent

9. The speaker first discussed several problems and then suggested **ingenious** solutions to all of them.

   ingenious (adj) – being very clever at making things or solving _____

10. The decision by the conference organizers to **impose** a ban on cell phones was very unpopular.

    impose (v) – force somebody to accept something, especially something unwanted or _____

D COMMUNICATE Work with a partner. Take turns responding to these questions.

1. If you could take the **ultimate** vacation, where would you go and what would you do?

2. Does your mood often **correlate** with what is happening in your life? Explain.

3. If people **generalize** about your country, what do they say? Are their views usually correct?

4. Have you ever attended a talk that **featured** amazing photos or other visuals? What was the topic of the talk?

5. What are some things that are **imperative** to do if you want to be successful?

6. Who is the most **ingenious** person you know? Support your opinion with examples.

WATCH

> learn**more** On TED.com, Wernicke's talk is described as "tongue-in-cheek." This adjective describes something that is intended to be humorous rather than serious. For example, it would be tongue-in-cheek for a teacher whose student always arrives late to class to suggest that this student should buy a new alarm clock or a new pair of running shoes.

E ▶ **1.41** **WATCH FOR MAIN IDEAS** Read these short summaries. Then watch segment 1 of the TED Talk. Check (✓) the summary that best describes the main focus of the talk. Then watch the complete talk and confirm your answer.

_____ **a.** Wernicke explains why making choices based purely on data can go wrong, and how a different approach might work better.

_____ **b.** Wernicke describes a method that he developed for summarizing every TED Talk in just six words.

_____ **c.** Wernicke gives a description of how statistical analysis let him come up with a way to generate the ultimate TED Talk.

NOTE-TAKING SKILL **Note Key Information on Slides**

Some speakers use slides when they give talks. In general, all the information on a slide is important, but sometimes a speaker will highlight certain key details—such as with an arrow, with animation, or by circling them. At other times, a speaker may change just a few details of the content when she switches to a new slide. If you see either of these things, make a note of the information that has been highlighted or changed.

F ▶ **1.42** **WATCH FOR DETAILS** Watch segment 2. As you listen, write one word in each blank to complete the notes.

Excerpt 1: *list of top 10 words in most fav. / least fav. TED Talks (TT) shows that*

popul. talk = French coffee spreads

_____ *in brains*

unpopul. talk = project about oxygen / girls /

_____

Excerpt 2: **1.** *spkr give service to* _____

= discuss what will give, <u>not</u> what cannot have

2. *should not mention NY Times*

3. *spkr can sound smart by saying*

_____

Excerpt 3: *color = close correl. with ratings of TT on*

_____

_____ *TT =* ↑ *blue than avg TT*

ingenious TT = ↑ _____ *than avg*

WORDS IN THE TALK
curated (adj): selected by somebody with a specific purpose
matrix (n): statistics or other data organized as a grid of rows and columns
props (n): physical objects that presenters show or use during talks

G ▶ **1.43** **WATCH AND RECOGNIZE THE SPEAKER'S ATTITUDE** Work with a partner. On the whole, Wernicke's talk is tongue-in-cheek, but at times he makes serious points. Look at the opening of his talk. Discuss which sentences he might say seriously. Then watch segment 3 to check his attitude in each sentence.

> *"There's a whole range of topics you can choose, but you should choose wisely, because your topic strongly correlates with how users will react to your talk. Now, to make this more concrete, let's look at the list of top 10 words that statistically stick out in the most favorite TED Talks and in the least favorite TED Talks. So, if you came here to talk about how French coffee will spread happiness in our brains, that's a go. Whereas, if you wanted to talk about your project involving oxygen, girls, aircraft—actually, I would like to hear that talk, but statistics say it's not so good. Oh, well."*

H ▶ **1.44** **WATCH FOR STRONGLY EXPRESSED VIEWS** Work with a partner. Add a phrase from the list to complete each excerpt from the talk. Two phrases won't be used. Then watch segment 4 to check your answers.

| I must | make sure | perfectly fine | vital to |
| it's imperative | most favorite | really important | you should |

1. *"First of all, _____, as a speaker, provide a service to the audience and talk about what I will give you, instead of saying what I can't have. Secondly, _____ that you do not cite the New York Times."*

2. *"And finally, it's OK for the speaker—that's the good news—to fake intellectual capacity. If I don't understand something, I can just say, 'etc., etc.' You'll all stay with me. It's _____."*

3. *"And analysis shows if you want to be among the _____ TED speakers, _____ let your hair grow a little bit longer than average, _____ you wear your glasses and be slightly more dressed-up than the average TED speaker."*

I **COLLABORATE** Work in a small group. Make a list of other phrases you can use to express your views strongly. Review the speaking skill box and exercise L on page 149 if you need some ideas.

J ▶ **1.45** **EXPAND YOUR VOCABULARY** Watch the excerpts from the TED Talk. Guess the meanings of the phrases in the box.

| stick out | that's a go | keep a sharp eye on |
| hold true | intellectual capacity | piece together |

AFTER YOU WATCH

K Work with a partner. Write each word in the correct space below. Then review exercise F on page 155 to confirm your answers.

> ingenious brains food color service
> ratings technical glasses oxygen inspiring

Wernicke's Tips for Giving the Ultimate Ted-Style Talk

TOPIC

- Words in popular TED Talks: French, coffee, _brains_ , happiness
  _1_
- Words in less popular TED Talks: _oxygen_ , girls, aircraft
  _2_
- Favorite talks cover topics that are easy to connect with, such as happiness, _food_ ,
  _3_
  emotions.
- Topics that are more _technical_ ,
  _4_
  such as architecture and materials are less popular.

DELIVERY

- Popular TED Talks are 50% longer than less popular ones. But talks that are beautiful, _inspiring_ , or
  _5_
  funny should be short.
- When talking, it is important to provide a _service_ to the audience.
  _6_
- Popular talks usually do not refer to the *New York Times*, but it is OK for speakers to say "etc. etc."

VISUALS

- Speakers of popular TED Talks wear _glasses_ , have longer
  _7_
  hair, and wear dressier clothes.
- It is OK to use either slides or props.
- _color_ is important and
  _8_
  correlates with the _ratings_
  _9_
  of talks on the Web site.
- Fascinating talks often use blue; _ingenious_ talks use
  _10_
  more green.

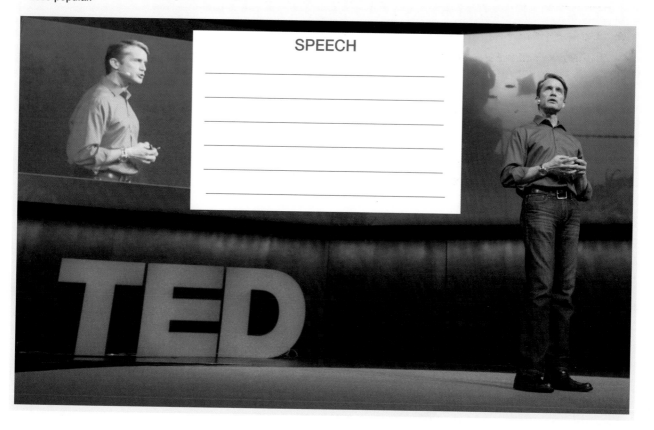

SPEECH

L THINK CRITICALLY Identify. Work in a small group. Wernicke does not mention speaking skills in his talk. Think about all of the TED Talks you have seen. Make a list of some of the speaking skills that the speakers used. Then share your list with the class. Decide which ones you find most useful and add them to the SPEECH section of the graphic on page 157.

> A: *I find that really good speakers pause often.*
>
> B: *Yeah, doing that helps the audience understand their ideas.*
>
> C: *And I find great speakers often use gestures and body language to emphasize key points.*

M THINK CRITICALLY Personalize. Work in a different small group. Even though Wernicke's talk is tongue-in-cheek, much of his advice is useful. Which of his suggestions will you try to use next time you give a talk, and which of his suggestions would be hard for you to adopt? Why?

> A: *Usually I wear contact lenses, but I might wear my glasses the next time I give a talk!*
>
> B: *What about people like me who don't need glasses or contacts?*
>
> C: *Why not wear some fake glasses?*
>
> B: *Now you're being tongue-in-cheek like Wernicke!*

N THINK CRITICALLY Identify. Work with a partner. What resources might help you learn to be a better speaker? Discuss some ideas and rank them from most useful to least useful. Then share your ideas with another pair of students.

> A: *Well, for me, watching vodcasts, or video podcasts, online has been a great resource.*
>
> B: *I agree. I've watched some, too. They can be on really interesting topics and they show a lot of different speaking styles.*

Put It Together

A **THINK CRITICALLY** **Synthesize.** Work in a small group. Read the information. Then discuss the questions.

> The idea worth spreading in Sebastian Wernicke's TED Talk is that analyzing data gives us information that can help us become better at many things, including giving presentations.

1. Does the example from Part 1 of the student who improved his life through self-tracking match Wernicke's idea worth spreading? Why, or why not?

2. Do these examples match Wernicke's idea worth spreading? Why, or why not?
   - Making a note of the most common mistakes you make in English in order to fix them
   - Thinking of things that cause you anxiety in order to work out some ways to avoid stress
   - Tracking how often you use social media in order to know how you spend your time online
   - Making a list of the foods you eat most often in order to decide if your diet is healthy or not

3. With your group, think of some more examples that would match Wernicke's idea worth spreading.

B **COMMUNICATE** Work in a different small group. Take turns responding to these questions.

1. What topics do you already have a lot of data or information about? How has it helped you?

2. What topics would you like more data about? Why? How would you get it? How might it help you?

COMMUNICATE

ASSIGNMENT: Give an Individual Presentation Talk about a time when you analyzed information to become better at something or discuss data you want to analyze so you can improve your life in some way. For instance, you could talk about how you analyzed your study habits in order to learn a subject more effectively or how you would like to track your expenses so as to save money. Review the ideas in Parts 1 and 2 and the listening and speaking skills as you prepare your presentation.

PREPARE

C Write a presentation outline in note form. Use these questions as a guide.

IF FOCUSING ON SOMETHING YOU HAVE *ALREADY* DONE	IF FOCUSING ON SOMETHING YOU *WILL* DO
• What information did you use? • How did you track or get the information? • How did you analyze it? • What actions did you take after your analysis? • How did your analysis make things better?	• What information do you need? • How could you get it? • How will you analyze it? • What actions might you take after the analysis? • What benefits do you hope the data will bring?
• Would you recommend that other people do the same kind of analysis? Why, or why not?	

> **PRESENTATION SKILL** Rehearse Your Talk
>
> Rehearsing will help you become more confident when you deliver your presentation. It will also help you with timing wording, and attracting and keeping your audience's attention. When you rehearse, follow some or all of these steps:
>
> 1. Rehearse your talk repeatedly until you are confident you can deliver it naturally and fluently.
>
> 2. Ask others to watch you rehearse. Ideally, ask at least one person who knows the subject of your talk well and one person who is unfamiliar with it. Listen to their feedback and adopt the best suggestions.
>
> 3. If possible, record yourself rehearsing. Then play back the recording and note things you could improve. (If recording yourself is not possible, rehearse in front of a mirror while you watch yourself.)

(See page 173 in the *Independent Student Handbook* for more information about rehearsing your talk.)

D **COLLABORATE** Work with a partner. Rehearse your presentation. Listen to your partner's feedback. Then watch your partner's rehearsal and give feedback. Think about the speaking skills you discussed in exercise L on page 158.

E **COLLABORATE** Work with a different partner. Rehearse your presentation again. Listen to your partner's feedback. Then watch your partner's rehearsal and give feedback.

F Read the rubric on page 182 before you present. Notice how your talk will be evaluated. Keep these categories in mind as you deliver your talk and watch your classmates' talks.

PRESENT

G Deliver your talk to a small group. Watch the talks of the other people in your group. Ask questions after each talk, if you wish.

H **THINK CRITICALLY** Evaluate. Work in the same small group. Share feedback on the presentations you watched and listen to feedback about your presentation. Say what you enjoyed most about presenting and listening.

REFLECT

Reflect on what you have learned. Check [✓] your progress.

I can
- [ ] listen for and recognize a speaker's attitude about something.
- [ ] strongly express my point of view about a topic.
- [ ] use stress and intonation to express comparisons and contrasts.
- [ ] note key information on slides.
- [ ] rehearse my talk in order to deliver it more effectively.

I understand the meanings of these words and can use them.
Circle those you know. Underline those you need to work on.

accumulate AWL	feature AWL	ingenious	statistical AWL
aspect AWL	generalize	interpret AWL	suffer
concrete	imperative	occur to AWL	technical AWL
correlate	impose	precise AWL	tempted
eligible	impressive	quantify	ultimate AWL

Independent Student Handbook

The *Independent Student Handbook* is a resource you can use during and after this course. It provides additional support for listening, speaking, note-taking, pronunciation, presentation, and vocabulary skills.

Listening Strategies

Predicting

Speakers giving formal talks usually begin by introducing themselves and then introducing their topic. Listen carefully to the introduction of the topic, and try to anticipate what you will hear.

Strategies:

- Use visual information including titles on the board, on slides, or in a PowerPoint presentation.
- Think about what you already know about the topic.
- Ask yourself questions that you think the speaker might answer.
- Listen for specific introduction phrases.

Listening for Main Ideas

It is important to be able to tell the difference between a speaker's main ideas and supporting details. In college, professors will often test students' understanding of the main ideas more than of specific details.

Strategies:

- Listen carefully to the introduction. The main idea is often stated at the end of the introduction.
- Listen for rhetorical questions, or questions that the speaker asks and then answers. Often the answer is the statement of the main idea.
- Notice ideas that are repeated or rephrased. Repetition and rephrasing often signal main ideas (see Common Phrases for Presenting, Repeating and Rephrasing, page 165).

Listening for Details (Examples)

A speaker will often provide examples that support a main idea. A good example can help you understand and remember the main idea better.

Strategies:

- Listen for specific phrases that introduce an example (see Common Phrases for Presenting, Giving Examples, page 165).
- Notice if an example comes after a general statement from the speaker.
- If there are several examples, decide if they all support the same idea.

Listening for Details (Reasons)

Speakers often give reasons or list causes and/or effects to support their ideas.

Strategies:

- Notice nouns that might signal causes/reasons (e.g., *factors, influences, causes, reasons*) or effects/results (e.g., *effects, results, outcomes, consequences*).

- Notice verbs that might signal causes/reasons (e.g., *contribute to, affect, influence, determine, produce, result in*) or effects/results (often these are passive, e.g., *is affected by*).

- Listen for specific phrases that introduce reasons/causes and effects/results (see Common Phrases for Presenting, Giving Reasons or Causes and Giving Results or Effects, page 164).

Understanding the Structure of the Presentation

An organized speaker will use certain expressions to alert you to the important information that will follow. Notice signal words and phrases that tell you how the presentation is organized and the relationship between main ideas.

Introduction

A good introduction includes something like a thesis statement, which identifies the topic and gives an idea of how the lecture or presentation will be organized. Here are some expressions to listen for that indicate a speaker is introducing a topic (see also Common Phrases for Presenting, Introducing a Topic, page 164):

I'll be talking about …

There are basically two groups …

My topic is …

There are three reasons …

Body

In the body of the lecture, the speaker will usually expand upon the topic. The speaker will use phrases that tell you the order of events or subtopics and their relationship to each other. Here are some expressions to listen for to help follow the body of a lecture (see also Common Phrases for Presenting, Listing or Sequencing, page 164):

The first / next / final (point) is …

Another reason is …

First / Next / Finally, let's look at …

However, …

Conclusion

In a conclusion, the speaker often summarizes what has already been said and may discuss what it means or make predictions or suggestions. Sometimes speakers ask a question in the conclusion to get the audience to think more about the topic. Here are some expressions to listen for that indicate a speaker is giving a conclusion (see also Common Phrases for Presenting, Conclusion, page 165):

In conclusion, …

As you can see …

In summary, …

To review, + (restatement of main points)

Understanding Meaning from Context

Speakers may use words that are new to you, or you may not understand exactly what they've said. In these situations, you can guess the meaning of a particular word or fill in the gaps of what you've understood by using the context or situation itself.

Strategies:

- Don't panic. You don't always understand every word of what a speaker says in your first language, either.

- Use context clues to fill in the blanks. What did you understand just before or just after the missing part? What did the speaker probably say?

- Listen for words and phrases that signal a definition or explanation (see Common Phrases for Presenting, Signaling a Definition, page 165).

Recognizing a Speaker's Bias

Speakers often have an opinion about the topic they are discussing. It's important for you to know if they are objective or subjective about the topic. Objective speakers do not express an opinion. Subjective speakers have a bias or strong feeling about the topic.

* Notice words like adjectives, adverbs, and modals that the speaker uses (e.g., *ideal, horribly, should, shouldn't*). These suggest that the speaker has a bias.
* Listen to the speaker's tone. Does he or she sound excited, happy, or bored?
* When presenting another point of view on the topic, is that other point of view given much less time and attention by the speaker?
* Listen for words that signal opinions (see Common Phrases for Classroom Communication, Expressing Opinions, page 166).

Common Phrases for Presenting

The chart below provides some common signal words and phrases that speakers use in the introduction, body, and conclusion of a presentation.

INTRODUCTION	
Introducing a Topic	
I'm going to talk about …	*Today we're going to talk about …*
My topic is …	*So we're going to show you …*
I'm going to present …	*Now/Right/So/Well,* (pause) *let's look at …*
I plan to discuss …	*There are three groups/reasons/effects/factors …*
Let's start with …	*There are four steps in this process.*

BODY	
Listing or Sequencing	**Signaling Problems/Solutions**
First/First of all/The first (noun)*/To start/To begin, …*	*The one problem/issue/challenge* (with) *is …*
Second/Secondly/The second/Next/Another/Also/ Then/In addition, …	*The one solution/answer/response is …*
Last/The last/Finally …	
There are many/several/three types/kinds of/ways, …	
Giving Reasons or Causes	**Giving Results or Effects**
Because + (clause): *Because it makes me feel happy …*	*so* + (clause): *so I went to the symphony*
Because of + (noun phrase): *Because of climate change …*	*Therefore,* + (sentence): *Therefore, I went to the symphony.*
Due to + (noun phrase) *…*	*As a result,* + (sentence).
Since + (clause) *…*	*Consequently,* + (sentence).
The reason that I like hip-hop is …	*… causes* + (noun phrase)
One reason that people listen to music is …	*… leads to* + (noun phrase)
One factor is + (noun phrase) *…*	*… had an impact/effect on* + (noun phrase)
The main reason that…	*If … then …*

Giving Examples	**Repeating and Rephrasing**
The first example is…	*What you need to know is …*
Here's an example of what I mean …	*I'll say this again, …*
For instance, …	*So again, let me repeat …*
For example, …	*The most important point is …*
Let me give you an example …	
… such as …	
… like …	
Signaling Additional Examples or Ideas	**Signaling to Stop Taking Notes**
Not only … but, besides	*You don't need this for the test.*
Besides …	*This information is in your books / on your handout / on the Web site.*
Not only do … but also	*You don't have to write all this down.*
Identifying a Side Track	**Returning to a Previous Topic**
This is off-topic, …	*Getting back to our previous discussion, …*
On a different subject, …	*To return to our earlier topic …*
As an aside, …	*OK, getting back on topic …*
That reminds me ….	*So to return to what we were saying, …*
Signaling a Definition	**Talking about Visuals**
Which means …	*This graph / infographic / diagram shows / explains …*
What that means is …	*The line / box / image represents …*
Or …	*The main point of this visual is …*
In other words, …	*You can see …*
Another way to say that is …	*From this we can see …*
That is …	
That is to say …	

CONCLUSION

Concluding	
Well / So, that's how I see it.	
In conclusion, …	
In summary, …	
To sum up, …	
As you can see, …	
At the end, …	
To review, + (restatement of main points)	

Common Phrases for Classroom Communication

The chart below shows some common phrases for expressing ideas and opinions in class and for interacting with your classmates during pair and group work exercises.

PHRASES FOR EXPRESSING YOURSELF

Expressing Opinions	**Expressing Likes and Dislikes**
I think …	*I like …*
I believe …	*I prefer …*
I'm sure …	*I love …*
In my opinion/view …	*I can't stand …*
If you ask me, …	*I hate …*
Personally, …	*I really don't like …*
To me, …	*I don't care for …*

Giving Facts	**Giving Tips or Suggestions**
There is evidence/proof …	Imperatives (e.g., *Try to get more sleep.*)
Experts claim/argue …	*You/We should/shouldn't …*
Studies show …	*You/We ought to …*
Researchers found …	*It's (not) a good idea to …*
The record shows …	*I suggest (that) …*
	Let's …
	How about + (noun/gerund)
	What about + (noun/gerund)
	Why don't we/you …
	You/We could …

PHRASES FOR INTERACTING WITH OTHERS

Agreeing	**Disagreeing**
I agree.	*I disagree.*
True.	*I'm not so sure about that.*
Good point.	*I don't know.*
Exactly.	*That's a good point, but I don't agree.*
Absolutely.	*I see what you mean, but I think that …*
I was just about to say that.	
Definitely.	
Right!	

PHRASES FOR INTERACTING WITH OTHERS

Clarifying / Checking Your Understanding

So are you saying that … ?

So what you mean is … ?

What do you mean?

How's that?

How so?

I'm not sure I understand/follow.

Do you mean … ?

I'm not sure what you mean.

Asking for Clarification/Confirming Understanding

Sorry, I didn't catch that. Could you repeat it?

I'm not sure I understand the question.

I'm not sure I understand what you mean.

Sorry, I'm not following you.

Are you saying that…?

Do you mean that…?

If I understand correctly, you're saying that …, right?

Oh, now I get it. You're talking about…, right?

Checking Others' Understanding

Does that make sense?

Do you understand?

Do you see what I mean?

Is that clear?

Are you following me?

Do you have any questions?

Asking for Opinions

What do you think?

We haven't heard from you in a while.

Do you have anything to add?

What are your thoughts?

How do you feel?

What's your opinion?

Taking Turns

Can I say something?

May I say something?

Could I add something?

Can I just say … ?

May I continue?

Can I finish what I was saying?

Would you finish what you were saying?

Did you finish your thought?

Let me finish.

Let's get back to …

Interrupting Politely

Excuse me.

Pardon me.

Forgive me for interrupting, …

I hate to interrupt, but …

Can I stop you for a second?

Asking for Repetition

Could you say that again?

I'm sorry?

I didn't catch what you said.

I'm sorry. I missed that. What did you say?

Could you repeat that, please?

Showing Interest

I see.

Really?

Um-hmm.

Wow.

Good for you.

Seriously?

No kidding!

And? (Then what?)

That's funny / amazing / incredible / awful!

Note-Taking Strategies

Taking notes is a personalized skill. It is important to develop a note-taking system that works well for you. However, there are some common strategies that you can use to improve your note taking.

BEFORE YOU LISTEN

Focus Try to clear your mind before the speaker begins so you can pay attention. If possible, review previous notes or what you already know about the topic.

Predict If you know the topic of the talk, think about what you might hear.

LISTEN

Take Notes by Hand

Research suggests that taking notes by hand rather than on a laptop or tablet is more effective. Taking notes by hand requires you to summarize, rephrase, and synthesize the information. This helps you *encode* the information, or put it into a form that you can understand and remember.

Listen for Signal Words and Phrases

Speakers often use signal words and phrases (see page 164) to organize their ideas and indicate what they are going to talk about. Listening for signal words and phrases can help you decide what information to write down in your notes.

> *Today we're going to talk about three alternative methods that are ecofriendly, fast, and efficient.*

Condense (Shorten) Information

- As you listen, focus on the most important ideas. The speaker will usually repeat, define, explain, and/or give examples of these ideas. Take notes on these ideas.

    Speaker: *Worldwide, people are using and wasting huge amounts of plastic. For example, Americans throw away 35 million plastic bottles a year.*

    Notes: *Waste plastic*
        Amer. 35 mil plastic bottles/year

- Don't write full sentences. Write only key words (nouns, verbs, adjectives, and adverbs), phrases, or short sentences.

    Full sentence: *The Maldives built a sea wall around the main island of Male.*

    Notes: *Built sea wall—Male*

- Leave out information that is obvious.

    Full sentence: *Van den Bercken fell in love with the music of Handel.*

    Notes: *VBD loves Handel*

- Write numbers and statistics. (*35 mil; 91%*)
- Use abbreviations (e.g., ft., min., yr) and symbols (=, ≠, >, <, %, ➞)
- Use indenting. Write main ideas on left side of paper. Indent details.

    Benefits of car sharing

    Save $

    Saved $300-400/mo.

- Write details under key terms to help you remember them.
- Write the definitions of important new words from the presentation.

AFTER YOU LISTEN

- Review your notes soon after the lecture or presentation. Add any details you missed and remember.
- Clarify anything you don't understand in your notes with a classmate or teacher.
- Add or highlight main ideas. Cross out details that aren't important or necessary.
- Rewrite anything that is hard to read or understand. Rewrite your notes in an outline or other graphic organizer to organize the information more clearly (see Organizing Information, below).
- Use arrows, boxes, diagrams, or other visual cues to show relationships between ideas.

ORGANIZING INFORMATION

Sometimes it is helpful to take notes using a graphic organizer. You can use one to take notes while you are listening or to organize your notes after you listen. Here are some examples of graphic organizers:

Flowcharts are used to show processes, or cause/effect relationships.

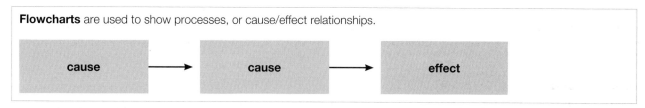

Mind maps show the connection between concepts. The main idea is usually in the center with supporting ideas and details around it.

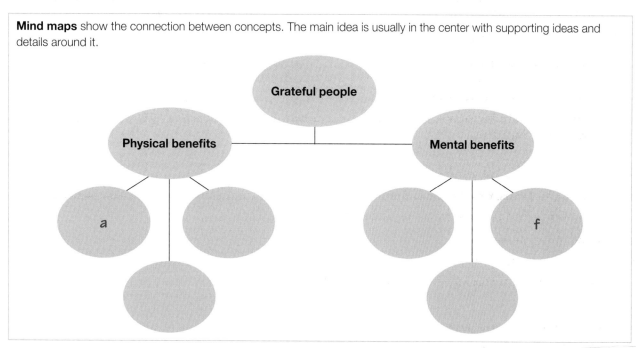

Outlines show the relationship between main ideas and details.

To use an outline for taking notes, write the main ideas starting at the left margin of your paper. Below the main ideas, indent and write the supporting ideas and details. You may do this as you listen, or go back and rewrite your notes as an outline later.

    I.   Saving Water

        A. Why is it crucial to save water?

            1. Save money

            2. Not enough fresh water in the world

T-charts compare two topics.

Hands-On Learning	
Advantages	**Disadvantages**
1. Uses all the senses (sight, touch, etc.)	1. Requires many types of materials
2. Encourages student participation	2. May be more difficult to manage large classes
3. Helps memory	3. Requires more teacher time to prepare

Timelines show a sequence of events.

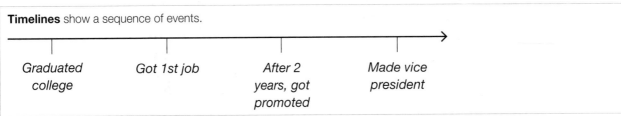

Graduated college   Got 1st job   After 2 years, got promoted   Made vice president

---

Venn diagrams compare and contrast two or more topics. The overlapping areas show similarities.

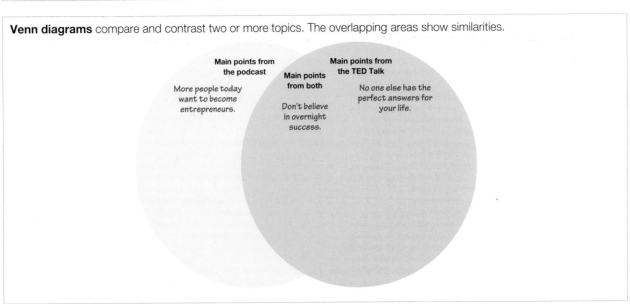

Main points from the podcast

More people today want to become entrepreneurs.

Main points from both

Don't believe in overnight success.

Main points from the TED Talk

No one else has the perfect answers for your life.

Pronunciation Strategies

When speaking English, it's important to pay attention to the pronunciation of specific sounds. It is also important to learn how to use rhythm, stress, and pausing. The charts below provide some tips about English pronunciation.

SPECIFIC SOUNDS

Vowels			Consonants		
Symbol	Key Word	Pronunciation	Symbol	Key Word	Pronunciation
/ɑ/	hot	/hɑt/	/b/	boy	/bɔɪ/
	far	/fɑr/	/d/	day	/deɪ/
/æ/	cat	/kæt/	/ʤ/	just	/ʤʌst/
/aɪ/	fine	/faɪn/	/f/	face	/feɪs/
/aʊ/	house	/haʊs/	/g/	get	/gɛt/
/ɛ/	bed	/bɛd/	/h/	hat	/hæt/
/eɪ/	name	/neɪm/	/k/	car	/kɑr/
/i/	need	/nid/	/l/	light	/laɪt/
/ɪ/	sit	/sɪt/	/m/	my	/maɪ/
/oʊ/	go	/goʊ/	/n/	nine	/naɪn/
/ʊ/	book	/bʊk/	/ŋ/	sing	/sɪŋ/
/u/	boot	/but/	/p/	pen	/pɛn/
/ɔ/	dog	/dɔg/	/r/	right	/raɪt/
	four	/fɔr/	/s/	see	/si/
/ɔɪ/	toy	/tɔɪ/	/t/	tea	/ti/
/ʌ/	cup	/kʌp/	/ʧ/	cheap	/ʧip/
/ɛr/	bird	/bɛrd/	/v/	vote	/voʊt/
/ə/	about	/əˈbaʊt/	/w/	west	/wɛst/
	after	/ˈæftər/	/y/	yes	/yɛs/
			/z/	zoo	/zu/
			/ð/	they	/ðeɪ/
			/θ/	think	/θɪŋk/
			/ʃ/	shoe	/ʃu/
			/ʒ/	vision	/ˈvɪʒən/

Source: *The Newbury House Dictionary plus Grammar Reference*, Fifth Edition, National Geographic Learning/Cengage Learning, 2014.

RHYTHM

The rhythm of English involves stress and pausing.

Stress

- English words are based on syllables—units of sound that include one vowel sound.

- In every word in English, one syllable has the primary stress.

- In English, speakers group words that go together based on the meaning and context of the sentence. These groups of words are called *thought groups*. In each thought group, one word is stressed more than the others—the stress is placed on the syllable with the primary stress in this word.

- In general, new ideas and information are stressed.

Pausing

- Pauses in English can be divided into two groups: long and short pauses.

- English speakers use long pauses to mark the conclusion of a thought, items in a list, or choices given.

- Short pauses are used between thought groups to break up the ideas in sentences into smaller, more manageable chunks of information.

INTONATION

English speakers use intonation, or pitch (the rise and fall of their voice), to help express meaning. For example, speakers usually use a rising intonation at the end of *yes/no* questions, and a falling intonation at the end of *wh-* questions and statements.

Presentation Strategies

You will often have to give individual or group presentations in your class. The strategies below will help you to prepare, present, and reflect on your presentations.

PREPARE

As you prepare your presentation:

Consider Your Topic

- *Choose a topic you feel passionate about.* If you are passionate about your topic, your audience will be more interested and excited about your topic, too. Focus on one major idea that you can bring to life. The best ideas are the ones your audience wants to experience.

Consider Your Purpose

- *Have a strong beginning.* Use an effective *hook*, such as a quote, an interesting example, a rhetorical question, or a powerful image to get your audience's attention. Include one sentence that explains what you will do in your presentation and why.

- *Stay focused.* Make sure your details and examples support your main points. Avoid sidetracks or unnecessary information that takes you away from your topic.

- *Use visuals that relate to your ideas.* Drawings, photos, video clips, infographics, charts, maps, slides, and physical objects can get your audience's attention and explain ideas effectively, quickly, and clearly. For example, a photo or map of a location you mention can help your audience picture a place they have never been. Slides with only key words and phrases can help emphasize your main points. Visuals should be bright, clear, and simple.

- *Have a strong conclusion.* A strong conclusion should serve the same purpose as the strong beginning—to get your audience's attention and make them think. Good conclusions often refer back to the introduction, or beginning, of the presentation. For example, if you ask a question in the beginning, you can answer it in the conclusion. Remember to restate your main points, and add a conclusion device such as a question, a call to action, or a quote.

Consider Your Audience

- *Share a personal story.* You can also present information that will get an emotional reaction; for example, information that will make your audience feel surprised, curious, worried, or upset. This will help your audience relate to you and your topic.

- *Use familiar concepts.* Think about the people in your audience. Ask yourself these questions: Where are they from? How old are they? What is their background? What do they already know about my topic? What information do I need to explain? Use language and concepts they will understand.

- *Be authentic (be yourself!).* Write your presentation yourself. Use words that you know and are comfortable using.

Rehearse

- *Make an outline* to help you organize your ideas.

- *Write notes on notecards.* Do not write full sentences, just key words and phrases to help you remember important ideas. Mark the words you should stress and places to pause.

- *Review the pronunciation skills* in your book. Check the pronunciation of words you are uncertain about with a classmate, a teacher, or in a dictionary. Note and practice the pronunciation of difficult words.

- *Memorize the introduction and conclusion.* Rehearse your presentation several times. Practice saying it out loud to yourself (perhaps in front of a mirror or video recorder) and in front of others.

- *Ask for feedback.* Note and revise material that doesn't flow smoothly based on feedback and on your own performance in rehearsal. If specific words or phrases are still a problem, rephrase them.

PRESENT

As you present:

- Pay attention to your pacing (how fast or slow you speak). Remember to speak slowly and clearly. Pause to allow your audience to process information.

- Speak at a volume loud enough to be heard by everyone in the audience, but not too loud. Ask the audience if your volume is OK at the beginning of your talk.

- Vary your intonation. Don't speak in the same tone throughout the talk. Your audience will be more interested if your voice rises and falls, speeds up and slows down to match the ideas you are talking about.

- Be friendly and relaxed with your audience. Remember to smile!

- Show enthusiasm for your topic. Use humor if appropriate.

- Have a relaxed body posture. Don't stand with your arms folded or look down at your notes. Use gestures when helpful to emphasize your points.

- Don't read directly from your notes. Use them to help you remember ideas.

- Don't look at or read from your visuals too much. Use them to support and illustrate your ideas.

- Use frequent eye contact with the entire audience.

REFLECT

As you reflect on your presentation:

- *Consider what you think went well* during your presentation and what areas you can improve upon.

- *Get feedback* from your classmates and teacher. How do their comments relate to your own thoughts about your presentation? Did they notice things you didn't? How can you use their feedback in your next presentation?

Vocabulary Learning Strategies

Vocabulary learning is an on-going process. The strategies below will help you learn and remember new vocabulary words.

Guessing Meaning from Context

You can often guess the meaning of an unfamiliar word by looking at or listening to the words and sentences around it. Speakers usually know when a word is unfamiliar to the audience, or is essential to understanding the main ideas, and will often provide clues as to its meaning.

- Repetition: A speaker may use the same key word or phrase, or use another form of the same word.

- Restatement or synonym: A speaker may give a synonym to explain the meaning of a word, using phrases such as, *in other words, also called, or …, also known as*.

- Antonyms: A speaker may define a word by explaining what it is NOT. The speaker might say *Unlike A / In contrast to A, B is …*

- Definition: Listen for signals such as *which means* or *is defined as*. Definitions can also be signaled by a pause.

- Examples: A speaker may provide examples that can help you figure out what something is. For example, *Paris-Plage is a* **recreation** *area on the River Seine, in Paris, France. It has a sandy beach, a swimming pool, and areas for inline skating, playing volleyball, and other activities.*

Understanding Word Families: Stems, Prefixes, and Suffixes

Use your understanding of stems, prefixes, and suffixes to recognize unfamiliar words and to expand your vocabulary. A stem is the root part of the word, which provides the main meaning. A prefix is before the stem and usually modifies meaning (e.g., adding *re-* to a word means "again"). A suffix is after the stem and usually changes the part of speech (e.g., adding *–ation / –sion / –ion* to a verb changes it to a noun). For example, in the word *endangered*, the stem or root is *danger*, the prefix is *en–*, and the suffix is *–ed*. Words that share the same stem or root belong to the same word family (e.g., *event, eventful, uneventful, uneventfully*).

Word Stem	Meaning	Example
ann (or *enn*)	year	anniversary, millennium
chron(o)	time	chronological, synchronize
flex (or *flect*)	bend	flexible, reflection
graph	draw, write	graphics, paragraph
lab	work	labor, collaborate
mob	move	mobility, automobile
sect	cut	sector, bisect
vac	empty	vacant, evacuate

Prefix	Meaning	Example
auto-	self	automatic, autonomy
bi-	two	bilingual, bicycle
dis-	not, negation, remove	disadvantages, disappear
inter-	between	Internet, international
mis-	bad, badly, incorrectly	misunderstand, misjudge
pre-	before	prehistoric, preheat
re-	again; back	repeat; return
trans-	across, beyond	transfer, translate

Suffix	Part of Speech	Example
-able (or *-ible*)	adjective	believable, impossible
-en	verb	lengthen, strengthen
-ful	adjective	beautiful, successful
-ize	verb	modernize, summarize
-ly	adverb; adjective	carefully, happily; friendly, lonely
-ment	noun	assignment, statement
-tion (or *-sion*)	noun	education, occasion
-wards	adverb	backwards, forwards

Using a Dictionary

A dictionary is a useful tool to help you understand unfamiliar vocabulary you read or hear. Here are some helpful tips for using a dictionary:

- When you see or hear a new word, try to guess its part of speech (noun, verb, adjective, etc.) and meaning, then look it up in a dictionary.

- Some words have multiple meanings. Look up a new word in the dictionary, and try to choose the correct meaning for the context. Then see if it makes sense within the context.

- When you look up a word, look at all the definitions to see if there is a basic core meaning. This will help you understand the word when it is used in a different context. Also look at all the related words, or words in the same family. This can help you expand your vocabulary. For example, the core meaning of *structure* involves something built or put together.

> **struc·ture** /ˈstrʌktʃər/ *n.* **1** [C] a building of any kind: *A new structure is being built on the corner.* **2** [C] any architectural object of any kind: *The Eiffel Tower is a famous Parisian structure.* **3** [U] the way parts are put together or organized: *the structure of a song‖a business's structure*
> —*v.* [T] **-tured, -turing, -tures** to put together or organize parts of s.t.: *We are structuring a plan to hire new teachers.* **-adj. structural.**

Source: *The Newbury House Dictionary plus Grammar Reference*, Fifth Edition, National Geographic Learning/Cengage Learning, 2014.

Multi-Word Units

You can improve your fluency if you learn and use vocabulary as multi-word units: idioms (*mend fences*), collocations (*trial and error*), and fixed expressions (*in other words*). Some multi-word units can only be understood as a chunk—the meaning of the phrase cannot be understood from the meaning of the individual words. Keep track of multi-word units in a notebook or on notecards.

Vocabulary Note Cards

You can expand your vocabulary by using vocabulary note cards. Write the word, expression, or sentence that you want to learn on one side. On the other, draw a four-square grid and write the following information in the squares: definition; translation (in your first language); sample sentence; synonyms. Choose words that are high frequency or on the academic word list. If you have looked a word up a few times, you should make a card for it.

definition:	first language translation:
sample sentence:	synonyms:

Organize the cards in review sets so you can practice them. Don't put words that are similar in spelling or meaning in the same review set, as you may get them mixed up. Go through the cards and test yourself on the meanings of the words or expressions. You can also practice with a partner.